# START NOW

# OR

# STAY STILL

## A JOURNEY TO GODLY DISCERNMENT

# START NOW

# OR

# STAY STILL

## A JOURNEY TO GODLY DISCERNMENT

## DAYNA THOMAS

# TABLE OF CONTENTS

# START NOW
# OR
# STAY STILL

## A JOURNEY TO GODLY DISCERNMENT

# PREFACE

It's really true, what people say, that when you are truly born again and see the truth of God, you can't keep it to yourself. Getting to know God for myself, and experiencing His consistency and divine intervention, ignited a fire in me to teach others about Him. What God planted in me is more than just sharing His Word. Simply *telling* people doesn't feel like enough. While I am still communing with God about this journey we are on together, He has made one thing clear. This book was next.

Before God revealed this book to me, He brought me to His feet to begin my journey of complete submission. It started when I filed for divorce after a short 16-month marriage. At that time, I had been a full-time entrepreneur for six years, and for the first time in my adult life, it felt like life was out of my control and going backwards; two very unfamiliar feelings. I remember thinking, *I just don't want to be depressed, I just don't want to be depressed.* I had never experienced depression before, but this situation felt like it could creep in. As a single mother to a four-year-old son (from a previous relationship), a law firm owner with a staff of eight, a talk show host, and a business coach to hundreds of lawyers and entrepreneurs, there was no room for depression. My strong mind had always been my greatest asset. It helped me build businesses, navigate challenges, and manage a full and demanding life. It was something I relied on, and I didn't want to lose it. The fear of slipping into depression is what ultimately drove me to seek God more seriously than ever before. I needed His help. I knew there was a way to get it, but I just didn't know how. So, I opened my Bible to find out.

Reading the Bible changed my life. I used to think (admittedly, in complete ignorance) that I didn't need to read the Bible "because God talks to me directly." While I could feel certain convictions, those subtle spiritual nudges are no replacement for the direct Word of God. I began to read the Bible daily, book by book, taking notes. I started with the epistles, then the Gospels, then went back to the beginning in Genesis and Exodus, and hopped around from there. I kept a running list of each book of the Bible I completed, and for each one, I took notes capturing the truths and promises revealed in the text. I felt like a child seeing the world for the first time. As I learned how God thinks, how He responds, what He expects, what He promises, and how He loves, it felt like I was meeting Him for the first time. But this time, I put Him in proper position: first.

What made the difference was that I began to respect the Bible as the truth, and not suggestions or advice. I chose to believe. That belief began to transform my behavior, or as I like to say, "how I show up in the world." I treated the Bible as a manual on how to live my life, and over time, the

Lord explained the Gospel to me by sparking questions in my mind that led me into deeper study, prayer, and understanding. My mind was renewed. I began to see people and situations differently, and I chose to surrender. For me, surrender meant releasing my future, and my expectations of how life should look, into God's hands. I became more aware of my thoughts and decisions, measuring them against the truth of God's Word. I chose to be bold and immediate in my transformation. Not perfect, but intentional. I still make mistakes, but now I take repentance seriously and refuse to entertain pride or the enemy. It's an all day, everyday commitment, but I have more peace and freedom than I've ever experienced.

And God restored, beyond anything I could have imagined. What once felt like going backwards now feels like being carried forward. I've learned that focusing daily on what God wants me to do *that day* creates space for Him to move. As my focus has shifted toward God rather than growing my law firm, my firm has become more profitable than ever before. I've lost count of how many new clients have told me "The Holy Spirit told me to call you." At first, I was surprised. Then I understood: God and I had an agreement. If I seek first His kingdom and His righteousness, everything else will be provided. (**Matthew 6:33**).

And it goes beyond just business. Everything has come together in a way that doesn't feel forced. Don't get me wrong—I've worked—but before this transformation, I worked much harder for far less, and without the level of peace and assurance I have now. When challenges arise, I am conscious to fight back with the truth of God's Word instead of reacting emotionally or even logically. I've watched God resolve things in ways I could never have orchestrated myself.

This transformation has impacted my family and relationships as well. I give more, serve more, and help more because I now understand that my supply is unlimited because my Father owns everything! I've realized that giving or disrupting my plans to help someone else will not deprive me of anything. When God directs my attention somewhere, I trust that He will make sure my home is taken care of, and He has.

This kind of freedom has brought me to my knees, face down in tears, overwhelmed with gratitude (I'm in tears even as I write this). The Lord saved me in more ways than one. Yes, I received salvation through Jesus Christ, but He also rescued me from how I used to think and live, and brought me right to Him. The joy, security, and freedom I now experience as a committed follower of Jesus are real.

My life before and after this transformation has shown me that we often struggle far more than necessary. That struggle comes from being attached to people, places, and outcomes, trying to hold everything together based on how we think it should be. That's exhausting! True freedom comes from surrender and being fully anchored in God. Out of His love, He allows us to enjoy what He's created, including the people in our lives. And when we keep Him first, He teaches us how to steward everything well with purpose and in peace. I couldn't keep this to myself. I wanted to be a vessel to help free my family, my friends, and anyone connected to me.

In 2023, while sitting alone having breakfast at a Bob Evans restaurant, the Lord gave me a vision. I saw myself on a platform, teaching His Word to a venue full of entrepreneurs. Instantly, I started tearing up, and I'm not even a crier! (I don't even feel like I can say that anymore because I cry more often now when I'm moved by the Holy Spirit). I kept saying out loud, "Okay Holy Spirit, I hear you! Please don't make me cry. I'm going to do it." That moment was the seed for *Paid in Full*.

A few months later, I launched *Paid in Full* with online bible studies and blogs to teach the Word of God, focusing on transformation, not just information. Through continued prayer and study, God made the mission clear: to help current and aspiring entrepreneurs out of struggle and into purpose through wholehearted surrender and devotion to God. What once felt unfamiliar became a priority.

In 2025, the Lord prompted me to lead a six-week online Bible study called *Start Now or Stay*

*Still.* The premise was to help entrepreneurs develop discernment to make decisions aligned with God's will. In full transparency, I delayed starting it. It felt like a big task that would require energy that I didn't think I had. But one day, I woke up and committed to begin. I started outlining the sessions, beginning with the idea that God prepares His people before He sends them. I continued the outline, feeling a bit unattached.

Then, unexpectedly as I was drafting the outline, I received an Instagram direct message notification on my phone. It was a voice note from Apostle Michelle Dejesus, whom I had met the year before and hadn't spoken to since. She shared that she woke up with me on her spirit and the Lord told her to message me. She said that she was hosting a 21-day 5 a.m. Bible bootcamp, and although there was a cost, the Lord told her to offer it to me for free. In that moment, I stopped working on my outline and decided to resume after the bootcamp.

Three weeks later, the vision was clear. I scrapped my original outline, and it was unmistakable that God was leading me to begin *Start Now or Stay Still* with teaching on covenants.

He revealed that true discernment cannot exist without a deep understanding of Jesus' sacrifice. Many have heard that "Jesus died for our sins," but what does that really mean, and why does it matter? Those questions became foundational.

I launched the *Start Now or Stay Still* online bible studies, and each week, God revealed the next lesson to me only after I completed the previous one, which was a true example of walking with Him (a concept you'll see unfold in Part III of this book). By the end of the six-week bible study, I felt like I had given birth spiritually. I thought it was finished, but a few weeks later, God gave me the instructions to turn those teachings into a book.

And here we are.

This book is an invitation into that same journey; one of truth, surrender, obedience, and transformation. It's not about perfection. It's about positioning your heart before God and allowing His Word and His Spirit to lead every area of your life. My prayer is that as you read, you don't just gain understanding, but that you encounter God for yourself. My hope is that your eyes will be opened, your mind renewed, and your life and desires become aligned with His will. If He did it for me, He will do it for you. All He requires is your yes.

<u>Note</u>: *This book is intended to help you engage with the Word of God and meant to be read with your Bible open beside you. Throughout these pages, you will find moments where you are prompted to stop and read specific Scriptures. I strongly encourage you to actually stop and read them, paying attention to the surrounding context. Write down questions, sit with what you read, and bring it to God in prayer for deeper understanding.*

# INTRODUCTION

## Understanding and Applying God's Word Will Change Your Life

Understanding the Word of God is not optional for the believer who desires to walk in true freedom, clarity, and spiritual authority. It is essential. Scripture makes it clear that hearing God's Word is only the beginning; understanding it is what causes the seed of truth to take root and flourish. In **Matthew 13:19**, Jesus warns that *"When anyone hears the word about the kingdom and doesn't understand it, the evil one comes and snatches away what was sown in his heart."* This reveals a powerful truth: without understanding, even the right message cannot produce the right results. The enemy targets what we do not understand because what we understand, we can apply, and what we apply, we can live.

Jesus expands on this in **Matthew 13:18–23** with the Parable of the Sower, illustrating the different responses people have to the Word of God. Some receive it with joy but quickly fall away because there is no root. Others allow the cares of the world or the deceitfulness of riches to choke what God has spoken. But those who hear, understand, and intentionally cultivate discernment, become "good soil." The Word says they produce fruit, sometimes thirtyfold, sixtyfold, even a hundredfold. Understanding is the difference between a life of frustration and a life of spiritual fruitfulness. It determines whether we are tossed by pressures, distracted by cares, or grounded enough to grow into everything God designed for us.

*Start Now or Stay Still* is a journey toward godly discernment. Discernment is what helps guide our lives in the way God intended, enabling us to make decisions rooted in love for Him and love for others. In doing so, it protects our divine purpose and directs us along the narrow road that leads to life as He designed it. Yet, clear and consistent discernment is nearly impossible in a life that is cluttered with distractions, driven by sin, and uninformed by the Word of God. True discernment begins with knowing the truth about who God is and understanding the meaning of what He has done for us through His Son, Jesus Christ. Building on this foundation, and being transformed by the truth of God's Word, leads to a meaningful life guided by the Holy Spirit.

God's kingdom operates in a divine order. We must first know the truth, which will shape our beliefs. What we believe will transform our behavior, and only then do feelings align. Satan works in reverse. He starts with manipulating our feelings to influence our behavior. The results of that behavior then shape false and limiting beliefs, which ultimately separate us from the truth.

When we understand the order of God's kingdom and how it works, we can confidently pursue His will without confusion or hesitation, walking in the provision, protection, and freedom that He promises. The truth is found in the Bible, and we must read it to plant the seed of truly knowing it. Once you discover the truth, you must accept it, even if it doesn't feel real or align with human logic. As your mind is renewed by what you know to be true, your beliefs begin to change, and you must challenge yourself to make decisions based on the truth (and it won't be easy). The results of those decisions ultimately shape the direction of your life. Jesus himself made it clear, "the truth will set you free."

This journey is not about speed. It is about alignment of our hearts, minds, and behaviors with God's truth so we can live the life He has already prepared for us.

*"The law, then, was our guardian until Christ, so that we could be justified by faith. But since that faith has come, we are no longer under a guardian, for through faith you are all sons of God in Christ Jesus."*

*Galatians 3:24-26*

Part One

THE COVENANTS
AND THE GOSPEL

# PART I

## The Covenants and The Gospel

### The First Covenant - Old Testament

A covenant—*diathēkē* in Greek—represents a sacred, binding arrangement. Unlike human agreements that may shift with circumstances, a covenant from God is intentional, unchanging, and anchored. The word *diathēkē*, used in the original text of the New Testament to refer to the First Covenant in the Old Testament, carries the meaning of a will, testament, or final disposition established with full authority and meant to remain valid. Covenants show us how seriously God takes His relationship with His people and how deeply

He desires to establish a lasting connection. When God forms a covenant, He reveals His heart, His promises, and His expectations.

One of the first covenants recorded in Scripture appears in the Old Testament, with God's promises to Abraham. God pledged to give Abraham's descendants land; specific, expansive, and strategically placed. **Genesis 15:18–20** details this promise with precision, listing territories from the Brook of Egypt to the Euphrates River, and naming the nations who occupied the land. But God's covenant was more than real estate. It was relational. In **Genesis 17:7–14**, He promised to be the God of Abraham and his offspring forever, calling it a *permanent covenant*. Circumcision served as the outward sign of this sacred agreement, symbolizing their commitment and distinguishing them as His covenant people. Any male who rejected this sign was considered to have broken the covenant, which was a serious breach that resulted in being cut off from the community.

**[<u>Stop and Read</u>: Genesis 15:18-20 and Genesis 17:7-14]**

In **Exodus 12:43–51**, God reaffirmed His covenant with Israel by reinforcing the necessity of circumcision for participation in the Lord's Passover, tying covenant protection to covenant identity. After the Israelites obeyed those instructions, **Exodus 12:51** says *"On that same day the Lord brought the Israelites out of the land of Egypt according to their military divisions,"* a demonstration of covenant faithfulness. God refers to this day in **Hebrews 8:9**, when he established his new covenant with humanity. (See page 26-27)

## The Covenant Continues

In **Exodus 19–24**, God deepened the covenant by giving Moses the Ten Commandments and a comprehensive set of laws covering justice, worship, community life, property, morality, and compassion. These laws (along with others found in Exodus, Leviticus, Numbers, and Deuteronomy) formed and established God's standard for holy living and provided structure for a new nation learning to walk with their covenant God. **Exodus 24:8** tells us that Moses sprinkled the blood of the covenant on the people, declaring, *"This is the blood* *of the covenant that the Lord has made with you concerning all these words,"* marking their formal acceptance.

**[<u>Stop and Read</u>: Exodus 19-24]**

## Warning and Judgment

But covenant blessing came with covenant responsibility. God made it clear that obedience would lead to protection, prosperity, and favor, while disobedience would bring consequences. **Deuteronomy 28:15** warns that failing to obey God's commands would result in curses overtaking the people. The seriousness of covenant commitment is emphasized again in **Deuteronomy 29:19–20**, where God warns against the dangerous mindset of believing one can follow a stubborn heart and still enjoy peace. Such rebellion invites judgment, not blessing. God's covenant was never meant to be taken lightly. It required wholehearted allegiance and trust.

Understanding the First Covenant (also known as the Old Covenant) matters for us today because it reveals God's nature, His standards, and

His unwavering commitment to those who walk with Him. It teaches us that God is a God of order, promise, and justice, and that relationship with Him is both a privilege and a responsibility. The framework of covenant lays the foundation for discernment, obedience, and spiritual maturity, preparing our hearts to appreciate the New Covenant established through Jesus Christ.

## The New Covenant - New Testament

### Why a New Covenant?

The Old Covenant, though sacred and revealed sin, could not remove it. **Hebrews 7:18–19** explains that the previous command was set aside because it was *"weak and unprofitable (for the law perfected nothing)..."* **Hebrews 10:11** further clarifies that in the days of the Old Covenant, *"Every priest stands day after day ministering and offering the same sacrifices time after time, which could never take away sins."* The law, therefore, was established to *"imprison everything under sin's*

**The Old Covenant, though sacred and revealed sin, could not remove it.**

*power"* (**Galatians 3:22**) and to be *"our guardian until Christ."* (**Galatians 3:24**). The Old Covenant paved the way for acceptance of the New Covenant, in which *"we are no longer under a guardian, for through faith you are all sons of God in Christ Jesus."* (**Galatians 3:25-26**).

God, in His love, provided a new and superior covenant of faith that allows us to draw near to Him, not through rituals or external signs, but through faith in Jesus Christ. The New Covenant stands at the center of God's redemptive plan, revealing both His love and His intention to restore humanity back to Himself.

## A Superior Covenant

A new covenant was necessary, not because God changed, but because His people needed a covenant that could change *them*. **Hebrews 8:7–13** (echoing **Jeremiah 31:31–34**) explains it:

> *"⁷For if that first covenant had been faultless, there would have been no occasion for a second one. ⁸But finding fault with his people, he says: See, the*

*days are coming, says the Lord, when I will make a new covenant with the house of Israel and with the house of Judah —* ⁹*not like the covenant that I made with their ancestors on the day I took them by the hand to lead them out of the land of Egypt. I showed no concern for them, says the Lord, because they did not continue in my covenant.* ¹⁰*For this is the covenant that I will make with the house of Israel after those days, says the Lord: I will put my laws into their minds and write them on their hearts. I will be their God, and they will be my people.* ¹¹*And each person will not teach his fellow citizen, and each his brother or sister, saying, "Know the Lord," because they will all know me, from the least to the greatest of them.* ¹²*For I will forgive their wrongdoing, and I will never again remember their sins.* ¹³*By saying a new covenant, he has declared that the first is obsolete. And what is obsolete and growing old is about to pass away."*

These verses explain that if the First Covenant had been faultless, there would be no need for another. The flaw was not in God's law, but in the people's inability to remain faithful. So God promised a covenant written not on stone tablets but on hearts, transforming His people from the inside out. Under this covenant, God pledges, *"I will be their God, and they will be my people,"* and He promises complete forgiveness, remembering their sins no more. And this new covenant is for all, as the Apostle Paul clarifies in **Galatians 3:27-29** *"For those of you who were baptized into Christ have been clothed with Christ. There is no Jew or Greek, slave or free, male and female; since you are all one in Christ. And if you belong to Christ, then you are Abraham's seed, heirs according to the promise."*

By establishing the New Covenant, God redeems transgressions committed under the Old Covenant (**Hebrews 9:15**), and replaces it with a relationship built on grace, intimacy, and the indwelling presence of His Spirit.

**[<u>Stop and Read</u>: Hebrews 8:7-13 and Jeremiah 31:31-34]**

## Making Way for the New Covenant

To move from the Old Covenant into the New, there had to be a death, because covenants (*diathēkē*) function like wills or binding agreements. A will can only be fulfilled when the one who

> The word "covenant" in Greek is *diathēkē* which means "a disposition, arrangement, of any sort, which one wishes to be valid, the last disposition which one makes of his earthly possessions, a testament or will; a compact, a covenant."

made it dies, and the same principle applies spiritually. According to **Hebrews 9:15-17**, Jesus became *"the mediator of a new covenant, so that those who are called might receive the promise of the eternal inheritance, because a death has taken place for redemption from transgressions committed under the first covenant. Where a will [diathēkē] exists, the death of the one who made it must be established. For a will is valid only when people die, since it is never in effect while the one who made it is living."* The text reveals that God, the maker of the First Covenant, had to die for that covenant (the will) to be fulfilled, thereby making room for a new one. Jesus, existing in the form of God, emptied and humbled Himself to the point of death on the cross. (**Philippians 2:5-8**).

## [<u>Stop and Read</u>: John 1:1-14 and Philippians 2:5-8]

The Old Covenant could not simply be canceled. It had to be fulfilled. In **Matthew 5:17**, Jesus makes it clear: *"Don't think I came to abolish the Law or the Prophets. I did not come to abolish, but to fulfill."* John the Baptist prophesies this fulfillment, declaring in **John 1:29** *"Look, the Lamb of God, who takes away the sin of the world!"* And Jesus confirms His assignment, expressing *"For this is my blood of the covenant, which is poured out for many for the forgiveness of sins."* (**Matthew 26:28**).

But according to the law, *"without the shedding of blood there is no forgiveness."* (**Hebrews 9:22**). Yet the blood of animals could never fully remove sin. **Hebrews 10:4** tells us plainly that *"it is impossible for the blood of bulls and goats to take away sins,"* which is why Jesus came declaring, *"I have come to do Your will."* (**Hebrews 10:9**). And *"By this will, we have been sanctified through the offering of the* *body of Jesus Christ once for all time."* (**Hebrews 10:10**). Through His sacrifice, *"He takes away the first to establish the second."* (**Hebrews 10:9**).

Jesus's offering, once and for all, achieved what repeated sacrifices of the Old Covenant never could. After making one perfect sacrifice for sins forever, He sat down at the right hand of God, signifying that the work was complete.

<u>**[Stop and Read</u>: Hebrews 9:1-28 and Hebrews 10:1-18]**

**The New Covenant - The Gospel!**

Humanity's universal condition is sin. *"For all have sinned and fall short of the glory of God"* (**Romans 3:23**), and sin carries a penalty we could never pay on our own. Out of love, God sent His Son, who is equal with God (**Philippians 2:6**), to die, be buried, and rise again so that we could be saved from that penalty and restored to Him. **John 3:16** declares that *"For God loved the world in this way: He gave his one and only Son, so that everyone who believes in him will not perish but have eternal life."* And **Colossians 2:14** certifies that *"He erased the* *certificate of debt, with its obligations, that was against us and opposed to us, and has taken it away by nailing it to the cross."* Through the New Covenant, God offers forgiveness, eternal life, and a reconciled relationship with Him to all who believe. *"For you are saved by grace through faith, and this is not from yourselves; it is God's gift — not from works, so that no one can boast."* (**Ephesians 2:8-9**). Praise God!

**Hebrews 2:14–15** reveals that Jesus shared in our humanity so that through His death He could destroy *"the one who had the power of death, that is, the devil,"* and free us from the fear that once held us in bondage. The Greek word used for "death" in this Scripture is *thanatos,* and carries the meaning of separation and misery in hell. (The original text of the New Testament was written in Greek.). But through Christ sacrificing his life on the cross, that fear and power are broken. We no longer live under condemnation, anxiety, or uncertainty. Instead, we

> **"For you are saved by grace through faith, and this is not from yourselves; it is God's gift — not from works, so that no one can boast."**
> **Ephesians 2:8-9**

walk in forgiveness, renewal, and freedom, living under the lordship of the One who overcame death—separation and misery in hell—on our behalf.

**How to Partake in the New Covenant**

Partaking in the New Covenant is beautifully simple, yet profoundly life-changing. Scripture makes clear that Christ brought an end to the law as the means of becoming righteous before God. Now righteousness is received through faith. (**Galatians 2:16**).

The New Covenant is for all. **Romans 10:9** teaches that *"If you confess with your mouth, "Jesus is Lord," and believe in your heart that God raised him from the dead, you will be saved."* It's a two-part endeavor, both equally important: 1) verbal confession, and 2) genuine belief. This belief is not merely intellectual agreement. It is a surrender of trust and control, placing our lives and confidence in Jesus rather than in our own efforts, goodness, or ability to earn God's approval. Through faith, we step fully into the promises and benefits of the New Covenant.

Entering the New Covenant life also means entering God's rest. **Hebrews 4:3** explains that *"we who have believed enter the rest,"* a Sabbath rest that still remains for God's people. This rest is not inactivity; it is release. It means ceasing from striving, from the pressure to create your own future, from the anxiety of trying to make everything happen by your own strength. Yet **Hebrews 4:11** acknowledges that entering this rest requires continuous effort. It can be very hard to let go, to believe beyond logic, to resist reacting from the flesh, and to obey when obedience feels costly. But as we *"make every effort to enter that rest"*, we learn to live from a place of trust, confidence, and surrender, experiencing the peace and stability that the New Covenant was designed to give.

**[Stop and Read: John 18-20 and Hebrews 4:1-11]**

> **"If you confess with your mouth, "Jesus is Lord," and believe in your heart that God raised him from the dead, you will be saved."**
> **Romans 10:9**

## Lord AND Savior – Not Just Savior

Receiving Jesus as *Savior* is only the beginning. The New Covenant calls us to receive Him as *Lord*; the One we obey, follow, and submit our lives to. Salvation is not a passive event, but an active transformation. **Hebrews 5:9** tells us that Jesus *"became the source of eternal salvation for all who* **obey** *him,"* and the Greek word for "obey" (*hypakouō*) carries the meaning of *submitting*. True salvation produces a posture of surrender, where our decisions, habits, and lifestyle come under the lordship of Christ. This obedience is not born out of fear or legalism, but out of love, because God's kindness is intended to lead us to repentance (**Romans 2:4**). Repentance means to change one's mind, direction, and behavior; to turn away from what pulls us from God and turn toward what draws us closer to Him.

Walking with God requires honesty about the areas of our lives that do not reflect Him. In my own journey, I started by writing down the things I was doing that I knew kept me out of alignment: fornication, arguing, watching movies and listening to music that glorify sin, cursing, and drinking alcohol. (Whew! Praise God for grace and deliverance!). These weren't just "bad habits." They were areas I had not yet surrendered to the leadership of Jesus, and He revealed more to me along the way. While the Bible tells us explicitly what thoughts and behaviors are sinful, God will also reveal to you personally what actions (or inactions) are keeping you distracted and hindered from elevation. For me, transformation began the moment I admitted them, repented, and submitted them to God. And this is exactly what His grace is designed to do.

**Titus 2:11–12** teaches that the grace of God not only brings salvation, but also *instructs* and *trains* us, thereby shaping us to renounce ungodliness and worldly passions, while empowering us to live self-controlled, upright, godly lives. Grace is both a gift and a teacher. Grace

"For the grace of God has appeared, bringing salvation for all people, instructing us to deny godlessness and worldly lusts and to live in a sensible, righteous, and godly way in the present age," Titus 2:11-12

doesn't excuse sin; it equips us to overcome it. Through obedience and surrender, we experience the fullness of Christ; not only as our Savior, but truly as our Lord.

## A Call to Salvation

If you're reading this and realizing that you haven't known Jesus as your Savior or fully surrendered to Him as your Lord, now is the perfect moment to respond. God is not looking for perfection. He is looking for a willing heart. His grace trains us, reshapes us, and empowers us, but that transformation begins with a decision: the decision to repent, surrender, and place your life under the authority and love of Jesus Christ. Salvation is not complicated. It is an invitation to step out of the old life, into the New Covenant, and into a relationship with God that transforms everything.

If you desire to make Jesus your Lord and Savior, or if you want to recommit your life to Him, pray this aloud with faith and sincerity:

> "Lord Jesus, I come to you
> admitting that I am a sinner.

> I repent of my sins and surrender my life to You. Wash me clean. I believe that Jesus Christ is the Son of God, that He died on the cross for my sins, and rose again on the third day. I am justified and made righteous through faith in Him. I believe in my heart and make confession with my mouth that Jesus is my Lord and Savior. I ask that You fill me with the power of the Holy Spirit. I receive eternal life, in Jesus' name, Amen."

If you made this declaration with a sincere heart, all of heaven rejoices and your journey of walking in truth, freedom, and discernment has truly begun. As you move forward, it is essential to get connected to a community of believers and be firmly planted in a Bible-based church, where you can grow, be supported, and remain rooted in the truth of God's Word. As an outward expression of your inward transformation, take time to inquire about baptism as a meaningful next step in publicly declaring your faith.

## Can You Lose Your Salvation?

One of the most common questions believers wrestle with is whether a person can lose their salvation. Scripture gives a sobering but nuanced answer. **Hebrews 6:4–6** and **Hebrews 10:26–27** warn that intentional, willful rejection of Christ after **receiving,** experiencing, and fully embracing the truth places a person in spiritual danger; not because salvation is fragile, but because they are *"recrucifying the Son of God."* (**Hebrews 6:6**). The Greek word for "receive" is *lambanō*, which means *to take hold of, claim, or appropriate for oneself.* This meaning goes far beyond merely *hearing* the Gospel. These passages refer to someone who has truly known Christ, tasted His goodness, shared in the Holy Spirit, and then deliberately turns away—an intentional renunciation, not an accidental stumble. **Hebrews 10:26-27** says *"For if we **deliberately** go on sinning after receiving the knowledge of the truth, there no longer remains a sacrifice for sins, but a terrifying expectation of judgment and the fury of a fire about to consume the adversaries."* Deeper study reveals that the word "deliberately" in Greek is *hekousiōs*, which means *to sin willfully as opposed to sins committed inconsiderately, and from ignorance or from weakness.* In other words, a person cannot "lose" salvation by mistake. It is forfeited through deliberate rejection. As I was studying this, the Spirit brought to mind the effect of voluntarily and with knowledge, signing a waiver of your rights.

What's even more sobering is how Scripture continues, stating in **Hebrews 10:28-29**, "*Anyone who disregarded the law of Moses died without mercy, based on the testimony of two or three witnesses. How much worse punishment do you think one will deserve who has trampled on the Son of God, who has regarded as profane the blood of the covenant by which he was sanctified, and who has insulted the Spirit of grace?*"

### [<u>Stop and Read</u>: Hebrews 6:4-12 and
### Hebrews 10:1-39]

Yet even with these warnings, Scripture immediately gives us reassurance: Jesus is our compassionate High Priest who is able to sympathize with our weaknesses and temptations. He invites us to approach the throne of grace boldly, where mercy and help are always available (**Hebrews 4:14–16**). These truths remind us not to live in fear, but to walk confidently with Christ; clinging to Him, trusting Him, and relying on His grace to help us in our time of need.

## Confession and Repentance

Another important truth in our walk with God is the power of confession. **1 John 1:9** says that *"If we confess our sins, he is faithful and just to forgive us our sins and to cleanse us from all unrighteousness."* In my own life, I've seen the spiritual protection that comes with confession and repentance. Nearly every time I verbally confessed my sins to God in prayer, that same night I would dream that something was trying to attack me—snakes, a burglar, bees, ninjas, a lion, a dog—yet none of them could touch or defeat me! Each time, the Holy Spirit reminded me that confession and repentance shield me from the enemy's attempts to harm or distract me. It was my confession and repentance that kept me protected from spiritual attacks.

Keep in mind that confession isn't a free pass, plan B, or an occasional prayer. It is a lifestyle of awareness, humility, and surrender. This lifestyle is strengthened by continuous and honest self-reflection and a commitment against internal pride. It's recognizing when your thoughts and actions don't align with the character or commandments of God, leading to you verbally acknowledge the wrong to Him in prayer. Confession feels good because it frees the soul. It brings a sense of relief and intimacy with God, while relieving the guilt and shame. As you confess, remember that Jesus does not expect perfection, but sympathizes with our weaknesses.

After you confess, repent. Repentance means to change one's mind and to turn with remorse from sin to God. So once you confess, you must turn away from that line of thinking or behavior. Both steps, confession then repentance, are critical. Your confession acknowledges that it's wrong, and your repentance commits to changed behavior. Again, this commitment does not mean perfection, but it is a standard that you are choosing to live by, and it does get easier.

In my own experience, I have found that after confessing and repenting of the same things multiple times, I've become more aware of those moments when the wrong choice presents itself. That awareness helps me choose God's way in the moment, knowing that if I don't, I will only find myself right back in confession and repentance again, so I've learned to choose better. That, over and over again, is a lifestyle. You start to become a different person, being more conscious about choosing things of God and refraining from thoughts and behaviors that don't represent Him. Confession and repentance isn't a meaningless cycle. It's a killer of pride, rooted in a sincere and grateful heart. It's not to be used as a recurring backup plan for deliberate sin, but rather a continuous posture of humility that produces transformation and honors Jesus's sacrifice to redeem us.

For many years, into my adult life, I didn't truly comprehend what it meant that "Jesus died for our sins." It sounded like a metaphor that no one could truly explain. But that's just it—no one can truly explain or deposit it in a way that will transform your life except God. God is the one who taught me what it means that Jesus died for our sins—over time, through His Word, and through His Spirit. He spoke, explained, showed me examples, allowed me to test what I learned, and confirmed. But first, I had to create space for Him to teach. I had to be a blank canvas and erase what the world taught me was real and make room for the actual truth. I had to eliminate my perception of morality and adopt a new definition of "good," defined by the character and commands of God. God coming here, humbling himself in the form of man, to live, die, and rise again, fulfilled the old covenant and made room for the new one, which took away the power of sin. By accepting Jesus as my Lord and Savior, a gift offered by grace and received through faith, I am made righteous and united with God, destined for eternal life. That same gift is available to us all.

Remember, you are not alone in this journey. God sent a helper, covering us every step of the way.

*"Now we have not received the spirit of the world, but the Spirit who comes from God, so that we may understand what has been freely given to us by God. We also speak these things, not in words taught by human wisdom, but in those taught by the Spirit, explaining spiritual things to spiritual people. But the person without the Spirit does not receive what comes from God's Spirit, because it is foolishness to him; he is not able to understand it since it is evaluated spiritually. The spiritual person, however, can evaluate everything, and yet he himself cannot be evaluated by anyone."*

1 Corinthians 2:12-15

# Part Two

## THE HOLY SPIRIT

# PART II

# The Holy Spirit

## The Gift of the Holy Spirit

When we receive salvation through Jesus Christ, we are not left to navigate our new life on our own. God gives us the Holy Spirit as a divine Helper, Counselor, Comforter, and Advocate. Jesus Himself promised this gift in **John 14:15–17**, explaining that those who love Him, shown through obedience, would receive *"another Counselor, to be with you forever. He is the Spirit of truth."* Unlike the world (those separated from God), which cannot receive the Holy Spirit, believers know the Holy Spirit because He not only walks with us, but lives *in* us. Jesus continued in

**John 14:25–26** by saying that the Holy Spirit would teach us all things and remind us of everything He said. This is one of the greatest assurances of the Christian life: we are never without access to guidance, power, or wisdom. The presence of the Holy Spirit is evidence that God did not merely save us; He equipped us.

## The Holy Spirit in the Old Testament

The Holy Spirit's work did not begin in the New Testament. Throughout the Old Testament, God placed His Spirit on individuals to empower them for His purposes. Othniel received the Spirit of the Lord to deliver Israel from oppression (**Judges 3:9–10**). Gideon was consumed by the Spirit of the Lord when he was called to lead Israel (**Judges 6:34**). The Spirit of the Lord rushed upon Samson, strengthening him to tear apart a young lion with his bare hands (**Judges 14:6**). Saul experienced a powerful move of the Spirit that enabled him to prophesy

This is one of the greatest assurances of the Christian life: we are never without access to guidance, power, or wisdom.

(**1 Samuel 10:10**). David was anointed and filled with the Spirit from the moment God chose him as king (**1 Samuel 16:12–13**). These examples show that God has always empowered His people through His Spirit, but under the New Covenant, this gift is not reserved for a few. The same Spirit who empowered warriors, kings, and prophets now dwells in every believer, equipping us to live, walk, and discern according to God's will.

## Truths and Characteristics of the Holy Spirit

As believers and followers of Christ, receiving the Holy Spirit is one of the greatest gifts of our salvation, yet many Christians live unaware of who He truly is or what His presence makes possible in our lives. We hear about the Holy Spirit in Scripture, we sense His guidance, and we may even feel His prompting, but understanding His identity and His role is essential for walking in discernment, power, and spiritual maturity. The Holy Spirit is not a distant force, an emotional experience, or a mystical concept. When we understand the truths about the Holy Spirit, such as who He is, how He works, and what He desires for us, our relationship with God deepens, our confidence grows, and our ability to walk in freedom becomes real. While this is not an exhaustive list of all there is to know about the Holy Spirit (an impossible feat), this section explores five foundational characteristics of the Holy Spirit so we can fully embrace the gift we have been given and live with the awareness that God Himself resides within us.

## #1 The Holy Spirit is God

The first truth every believer must understand about the Holy Spirit is that He is God. From the very beginning of Scripture, we see hints of God's triune nature. In **Genesis 1:26**, God says, *"Let us make man in our image,"* revealing plurality within the Godhead even at creation. Jesus affirms this in **Matthew 28:19** when He commands His disciples to baptize *"in the name of the Father and of the Son and of the Holy Spirit."* The Holy Spirit is not an optional add-on, an energy, or a lesser divine force. He is the third person of the Trinity, fully God in essence and authority. Although the mystery of one God in three persons may challenge our understanding, our faith is not dependent on our ability to fully comprehend God, but on trusting who He reveals Himself to be. And while we refer to Him as the "third" person of the Trinity, that designation speaks to order, not rank. The Holy Spirit is not last, least, or lower inside the Godhead. He is equal with the Father and the Son, worthy of honor and obedience.

## #2 The Holy Spirit Lives in You

The second essential truth is that the Holy Spirit lives in you. Through salvation, every believer receives the indwelling Spirit, who is God Himself taking residence within us. Paul reminds Timothy of this when he says, *"Guard the good deposit through the Holy Spirit who lives in us"* (**2 Timothy 1:14**). Likewise, **1 Corinthians 6:19** declares that our bodies are temples of the Holy Spirit, emphasizing that He is not simply *with* us; He is *within* us. You don't "catch" the Holy Spirit like a feeling, an emotional moment, or a church atmosphere. His presence is not something that comes and goes. He is a permanent resident. If we truly believed that, many of our choices, behaviors, and compromises would look very different. The real question is not whether you have the Holy Spirit (because if you are saved, you do) but **does the Holy Spirit have you?** Does He have your obedience, your thoughts, your desires, and your willingness to be led? Understanding His presence within you is the foundation of discernment, transformation, and spiritual authority.

## #3 The Holy Spirit Requires Attention

A third important truth about the Holy Spirit is that He requires your attention. The Spirit does not force Himself on us or override our choices. Instead, He leads, prompts, warns, comforts, and guides, but we must intentionally tune our minds and hearts to Him. **Romans 8:5–6** makes this clear: *"For those who live according to the flesh have their minds set on the things of the flesh, but those who live according to the Spirit have their minds set on the things of the Spirit."* The difference between spiritual life and spiritual death is found in the mindset. Though we are no longer slaves to sin and have been given the Holy Spirit to overcome our old nature, we must choose daily whether our thoughts will rest on worldly desires or on the things of God.

This requires honesty and frequent self-examination. Ask yourself: *Why do I want this? Why am I upset? Why am I pursuing this relationship? Why do I choose alcohol? Why do I want to quit on my business? Why can't I let go of this thing/person that is hurting me? Why do I want to post this?* These questions help reveal whether your mind is aligned with the Spirit of God or drifting toward your flesh. But this only works to guide you in the Spirit if you are truly honest. Every day you are faced with choices and moments where you can either "start now" by following the Spirit's direction or "stay still" in patterns that keep you stuck. Likewise, you may "start now" out of haste and human impulse, or "stay still" in disciplined obedience, trusting God's timing over your own. The Holy Spirit is always speaking, but we must create space to listen; not just emotionally, but intentionally. Slow down. Pause. Acknowledge Him. Talk to Him. Listen for His direction instead of rushing into decisions led by impulse or pressure. And when He reminds you of the truth, stand on it firmly. Walking with the Holy Spirit is not a moment. It's a lifestyle built on awareness, intentionality, humility, and consistent surrender.

## #4 The Holy Spirit Knows EVERYTHING

A fourth essential truth is this: the Holy Spirit knows everything. **1 John 2:20** says *"But you have an anointing from the Holy One, and all of you know the truth."* This doesn't mean we instantly understand all things intellectually. It means the Holy Spirit within us teaches, reveals, and confirms truth in our hearts. **1 John 2:27** reinforces this by saying *"As for you, the anointing you received from him remains in you, and you don't need anyone to teach you. Instead, his anointing teaches you about all things and is true and is not a lie; just as it has taught you, remain in him."* Jesus echoed this promise in **John 16:13**, explaining that *"When the Spirit of truth comes, He will guide you into all truth. For he will not speak on his own, but he will speak whatever he hears. He will also declare to you what is to come."* The truth that the Spirit reveals is always consistent with the Word of God the Father and the Son, Jesus Christ. He does not act independently or invent new rules or doctrines. His guidance will always align with Scripture and the character of God.

However, for the Holy Spirit's guidance to be clear in our lives, we must be honest about our intentions. The Spirit reveals truth, but if our hearts are committed to our own desires, we may mistake our feelings for His voice. This is where many believers struggle.

In my own life, I experienced this when it came to marriage. I wanted to be married and have a family of my own so badly that I convinced myself that God approved of my boyfriend at the time, even though I didn't truly consider God in my decision. My longing led me to adopt a false narrative: *"This is the next step that God has for me."* But the truth was that I wanted to build *my* vision for my life, regardless of what God thought about it. Unsurprisingly, that marriage quickly ended in divorce, but thankfully, God's grace in my disobedience brought me to my knees in true surrender to Him.

This is why honesty with God (and with ourselves) is essential. Because the Holy Spirit, who lives within us who are saved, knows all things, we already have access to the answers for every problem and question we face in life, but He will not override our stubborn self-deception. As we remain grounded in the Word of God, honest and humble in self-reflection, and obedient to the Holy Spirit's promptings, we become better able to hear His guidance and clearly discern the right path.

## #5 The Holy Spirit *is* the Power

You must understand that the Holy Spirit is not merely powerful. He *is* the power of God at work within you. **Romans 8:11** declares that the same Spirit who raised Jesus from the dead lives in every believer. This means world-shaking, death-defeating, and life-giving power dwells inside of you! Not visits you. Not occasionally touches you. Lives in you!

**2 Peter 1:3** echoes this, reminding us that God's divine power has already given us *everything* required for life and godliness. Nothing you need to live the life God designed for you is missing. The Holy Spirit supplies strength when you are weak, clarity when you are lost, and endurance when you feel like giving up.

Even Jesus, God in the flesh, relied on the Holy Spirit. **Luke 4:1–2** shows Jesus entering the wilderness *"full of the Holy Spirit"* before facing

Satan's temptations. The enemy tempted Jesus with food, power, identity, and Scripture itself, but Jesus overcame because He was led and strengthened by the Spirit. The same Spirit who empowered Jesus empowers you. The same Spirit who came upon Samson and enabled him to tear apart a lion (**Judges 14:6**) enables you to conquer the "impossible" situations in your life. The Holy Spirit is your strength in your lowest and weakest moments, the One who sustains you when life feels like a wilderness and you don't know what to do. The enemy waits until you are tired, frustrated, or overwhelmed, but even then, the Spirit intercedes, helps you, lifts you, and keeps you from falling. **2 Timothy 1:7** declares *"For God has not given us a spirit of fear, but one of power, love, and sound judgment."* You must use your divine power, but you can't use it if you don't believe you have it.

The Holy Spirit not only strengthens you, He also convicts you and leads you into truth. Jesus said in **John 16:7–8** that the Spirit would come as a Helper, Counselor, Comforter, Advocate, and Intercessor, bringing light to areas that need correction and guiding you into righteousness. His conviction is not condemnation. It is protection and a loving course-correction meant to keep you aligned with God's will. And because He is your Helper, you never have to face life in your own strength again. **Hebrews 13:6** boldly declares, *"The Lord is my helper; I will not be afraid. What can man do to me?"* With the Holy Spirit as your power, your teacher,

You are saved by Christ, sealed by the Father, and strengthened by the Spirit.

your guide, and your strength, you can walk confidently into every season knowing that God Himself is working within you, shaping you, empowering you, and sustaining you every step of the way.

This truth completes the picture. You are saved by Christ, sealed by the Father, and strengthened by the Spirit. Nothing about your walk with God depends on your own ability apart from Him. You were never meant to do this life by yourself. If we connect with the power that lives within us, we can defeat the façades that the world presents as real. Separating what's real and true from the lies is a pillar of godly discernment.

## Respond to the Holy Spirit

Don't just *feel* the Holy Spirit; respond to Him. Let this be the moment you decide to take intentional steps toward a deeper, more Spirit-led life. Start by **confessing your sins and repenting**. Bring everything, past and present, into the light, including your habits, your struggles, your attitudes, and your attachments. Confession isn't for God's information; it's for your freedom. Repentance (turning away from your sin) clears the static so you can hear the Holy Spirit clearly and walk in the purity and power He desires for you.

Begin cultivating a relationship with God by **talking to the Holy Spirit daily**. In the morning, ask Him for guidance. Throughout the day, ask for help, wisdom, strength, and clarity. He is not distant. He is present, willing, and eager to lead you in all things. Let Him guide your decisions, emotions, thoughts, and routines. Verbally invite Him into your moments, both big and small.

And finally, **create a space in your home dedicated to your communion with God**. A place where you meet with Him, pray, hear His voice, journal, worship, cry, and rest in His presence. It doesn't have to be big or fancy. It just needs to be yours. And it's not your only place for prayer, but it's set apart. Let this be your personal altar where you release your burdens, confess, and repent. It's your dedicated special place, away from distractions so you can focus on His presence and His response. Here, let the Holy Spirit shape you, strengthen you, and train you in discernment. As you confess, converse, and commune with Him, you will grow in spiritual sensitivity, clarity, and confidence, living every day aware that God Himself is with you, in you, and guiding your every step.

*"So then, just as you have received Christ Jesus as Lord, continue to walk in him, being rooted and built up in him and established in the faith, just as you were taught, and overflowing with gratitude."*

Colossians 2:6-7

# Part Three

## WALKING WITH GOD

# PART III

## Walking with God

### Walking – A Scriptural Motif

Walking with God is not just a spiritual concept; it is a lifestyle, a daily posture, and a deliberate choice. Scripture calls us to this *walk* again and again. In **Ephesians 4:1–3**, Paul urges believers to *"**walk** worthy of the calling you have received,"* marked by humility, gentleness, patience, and love. This walk requires effort, unity, and peace. It is intentional, not accidental. Paul also counsels us to *"**walk** by the Spirit and you will certainly not carry out the desires of the flesh"* (**Galatians 5:16**). In other words, when we consistently follow the leading of the Holy Spirit, our desires, decisions, and actions begin to align more with God's will than our natural impulses.

In **1 John 1:7**, the Apostle John encourages that *"If we **walk** in the light as he himself is in the light, we have fellowship with one another, and the blood of Jesus his Son cleanses us from all sin."* **Proverbs 16:9** says, *"a person's heart plans their way, but the Lord determines their **steps**."* We can dream, plan, and strategize, but God is the One who directs. And **2 Corinthians 5:7** anchors this truth even deeper: *"For we **walk** by faith, not by sight."*

Notice the common ground: **walking**. God is not asking us to sprint, rush, or hurry blindly into the future. Most people want God to show them the entire plan now, so they can take off running. Many don't even take the first step until they can see how it's all going to work out. But God asks us to walk. One step at a time. One instruction at a time. One act of obedience at a time. Walking with God means trusting His direction even when the path is not fully revealed, moving steadily instead of hastily, and letting faith (not feelings) guide your steps.

## The Nature of Walking with God

As we learn to walk with God, we must remember that we are not doing this alone. **Philippians 2:13** assures us, *"For it is God who is working in you both to will and to work according to His good purpose."* **Galatians 5:25** says, *"If we live by the Spirit, let us also keep in step with the Spirit."* God doesn't simply give us commands and leave us to figure them out. He shapes our desires, strengthens our actions, and guides our steps. But it will be hard to discern your path if you are unaware of God's nature and values. Through reading the Bible, we learn the patterns and principles of how He leads. These patterns are not formulas or rules, but characteristics and principles that help us recognize His leadership, trust His timing, and respond to His voice. As you grow spiritually, these traits become anchors, reminding you of who God is, how He works, and how He guides His people.

The following eight elements reveal the nature of walking with God, helping you understand what it looks like in your everyday life, step by step, with confidence and clarity.

## #1. God's Timing is Not Your Timing

One of the most challenging lessons in walking with God is accepting that His timeline rarely matches ours. We want things fixed now. We want answers now. We want a breakthrough now. But walking with God means trusting His timing even when waiting feels uncomfortable. Scripture gives us powerful examples of this. Joseph waited about twenty-two years from receiving his dream of authority to seeing it fulfilled (**Genesis 37-45**). David was anointed as king when he was only a teenager (historical estimates deem around fifteen to seventeen years old) but did not actually become king of all Israel until he was thirty years old (**1 Samuel 16 - 2 Samuel 5**). During those years of waiting, he fought physical battles, ran from the lethal jealousy of King Saul, lived in the wilderness to hide, and endured season after season that felt nothing like a promise. Yet, God's word to David was still true, even in the waiting. The same is true for you. God will do what He said He will do. Your responsibility is to walk with Him, trust His timing, and hold onto the promise, faithfully, until it comes to pass.

## #2. God Doesn't Show You the Whole Plan

God rarely reveals everything at once. **Proverbs 16:3** tells us, *"Commit your activities to the Lord, and your plans will be established."* Notice the order. You commit, then He establishes. God often gives us one instruction at a time, and as we obey, He reveals more. We see this clearly in the life of Abraham (who God renamed, Abram). In **Genesis 12:1,** God tells Abram, *"Go from your land, your relatives, and your father's house to the land that I will show you."* Not *have shown you.* Not *described in detail.* God instructed Abraham to move before He even revealed the destination. Along with the instruction to Abraham came promises, blessings, protection, favor, and purpose, but the specifics unfolded only as Abraham walked.

### [Stop and Read: Genesis 12:1-9]

The same pattern shows up in Samuel's story. In **1 Samuel 16:1-3**, God tells Samuel to go to Bethlehem because He has chosen a new king among Jesse's sons. Samuel fears King Saul's reaction and asks how he can go without being killed. God responds by giving him a strategy: take a sacrifice, invite Jesse, and *then,* God says, *"I will let you know what you are to do."* Samuel did not receive the full plan upfront. He received the next step and the wisdom to navigate it safely.

This is how God works with us as well. Many believers wait for God to lay out the entire plan before they even take one step; but if He did, most of us wouldn't go. The magnitude would overwhelm us, or the future challenges would intimidate us. God reveals the plan *progressively* because He is preparing us along the way, shaping our character, strengthening our faith, and teaching us to trust His voice more than our understanding. Walking with God means trusting that He has a pace and plan, even when the whole picture isn't clear, believing that He never leaves us without the guidance and strategy we need for each step.

## #3. Move When God Says Move

Walking with God requires obedience. Not delayed obedience or partial obedience, but willingness to move when He says move. In **1 Samuel 10:7**, after Saul was anointed, Samuel told him, *"When these signs have happened to you, do* *whatever your circumstances require because God is with you."* In other words: *When God confirms His direction, respond boldly.* Walking with God means being willing to do whatever it takes to follow His lead, even when the details are not fully clear upfront. Jesus emphasized this principle in **Luke 11:28**: *"Blessed are those who hear the word of God and keep it."* Hearing is not enough. Obedience matters, and it activates your blessing.

Scripture also confronts our tendency to stall. In **Joshua 18:3**, Joshua asks the tribes of Israel, *"How long will you delay taking possession of the land the Lord of your ancestors gave you?"* God had already granted the promise, but the Israelites were hesitating, waiting, and delaying. Many believers still do the same today. God says "go," but we wait for perfect conditions. God says "start," but we wait for more clarity. God says "move," but we linger in fear or uncertainty. However, we must believe that when God gives instruction, He also provides the pathway. **Proverbs 16:7** assures us that when our ways please the Lord, *"He makes even our enemies to be at peace with us."* If God is leading you to do something, He will make a way for it, aligning circumstances, shifting hearts, and opening doors no one can shut. He will make people get in formation! Walking with God means trusting that if He spoke it, He will support it. Move when God says move, and watch Him orchestrate everything you cannot.

## #4. Understand That it May Not Make Sense to You

Walking with God requires trust even when His instructions defy logic. **Proverbs 3:5–6** tells us, *"Trust in the Lord with all your heart and lean not on your own understanding; in all your ways acknowledge Him, and He will direct your paths."* God's guidance often won't fit into our natural reasoning. It won't always be logical, predictable, or comfortable, and it's not meant to be, because walking with God is a walk of faith. His power goes beyond what we can see, calculate, or control. If life with God always made sense, we would never need to rely on Him. We must refrain from doubting God because something doesn't make sense to us. Our human brain doesn't even have the capacity to think of the solution He will present. In **Proverbs 3:5-6**, we are directed to acknowledge Him in all things, and the promise is that He will guide us.

Bear in your heart and mind that God's directions, no matter how uncertain or uncomfortable they may seem, are rooted in wisdom and love. In **Exodus 13:17–18** when God freed the Israelites from slavery in Egypt, He did not lead them on the shorter route to the Promised Land. Instead, He took them the long way around, toward the Red Sea. God's instruction didn't seem to make sense geographically, but Scripture explains why he made that decision: God knew the shorter route meant confronting the Philistines in war, which was something the Israelites weren't ready for, and that fear would have driven them back to Egypt. So He led them to the Promised Land through a different route, which was longer, but protected the promise that God made to Abraham (*"To your offspring, I will give this land."* **Genesis 12:7**). This demonstrates that God leads us according to what we can handle, what will strengthen us, and what will ultimately bring us into His purpose. If God immediately granted everything we thought we wanted, we would settle for a life far beneath the one He designed for us. To the limited human mind, the path to the Red Sea seemed like a fatal dead end, until God miraculously parted the waters. (**Exodus 14:10-31**). The same is true in our lives. God leads us exactly where we need to be so He can show His power in ways we never imagined.

Sometimes God's instructions don't make sense until we understand that He can do more with less. Gideon's story in **Judges 7** proves this. Gideon began with 30,000 soldiers, but God reduced his army to just 300 so that Israel couldn't claim victory by their own strength. When those 300 soldiers blew their horns in battle, God caused the Midianites (an army too large to count) to turn their swords against each other. No one could have predicted God's strategy. Similarly today, we often think we need more before we can start doing what God told us to do: more money, more connections, more resources, more time, etc. But the Bible reveals that God delights in showing His strength through what seems insufficient.

**[<u>Stop and Read</u>: Judges 7:1-23]**

In **Numbers 11:1-32,** God provided meat (a luxurious meal) for the Israelites on their trek to the Promised Land, not for one day, but for thirty days and for over 600,000 men. The Israelites doubted, unable to imagine how God could provide that much. Even Moses doubted, boldly questioning if there would be enough meat for everyone if flocks and herds were slaughtered, and all the fish in the sea were caught. God responded to Moses's doubt with a rhetorical question, *"Is the Lord's arm weak?"* (**Numbers 11:23**), then sent a wind that brought quail in such abundance that even the person who gathered the least collected about sixty bushels.

### [<u>Stop and Read</u>: Numbers 11:1-32]

God's ways will not always make sense, but they will always be sufficient. He will do things in ways that you cannot predict, think of, or imagine, but you can always trust Him to deliver.

## #5. Disobedience Leads to Delay

One of the most sobering truths in walking with God is that disobedience doesn't just grieve the heart of God, it is an offense towards God and delays your promise. **James 4:17** puts it plainly: *"So it is sin to know the good and yet not do it."* In other words, sin is not only doing what is wrong; it's also refusing to do what you know is right. Ask yourself honestly: *What should I be doing that I'm not doing?* Are you avoiding spending time in Scripture? Neglecting prayer? Leaving things unresolved when you know you're wrong? Ignoring the nudges to work on your business, start the program, finish the book, launch the event, or help someone else with what they are building? Your obedience isn't just about you. Other people are connected to your 'yes.'

Likewise, ask: *What should I stop doing that I continue to entertain?* Arguing with people, holding grudges, cutting corners financially, choosing low integrity actions, staying in toxic relationships, giving your body to someone you're not married to, getting drunk, or making reckless decisions. These behaviors don't just harm you physically, mentally, and emotionally, they hinder your progress and promotion.

But how do we actually know right from wrong? God guides us through two primary sources: His Word and His Spirit. Scripture gives us instruction for life. When Joshua took leadership after Moses, God told him, *"This book of instruction must not depart from your mouth; you are to meditate on it day and night so that you may carefully observe everything written in it. For then you will prosper and have success in whatever you do."* (**Joshua 1:8**).

The Bible teaches us how to move and make decisions in everyday life, such as how to interact with people, handle money, resist temptation, and guard our integrity, to name a few. For example, in my own life, Scripture guided my attitude when someone failed to repay a loan. **Luke 6:35** tells us to *"lend, expecting nothing in return,"* meaning we should release resentment and not let unpaid debts harden our hearts. But this does not excuse the borrower's responsibility. **Psalm 37:21** says plainly, *"The wicked person borrows and does not repay."* In other words, forgiving a debt does not make it right for the borrower to ignore it. The lender is called to let go of the offense, but the borrower is still accountable before God for repaying what they owe. This is the balance of Scripture; grace required of the giver, and integrity required of the borrower.

There are countless examples of God's Word showing us how to act and react in a variety of situations that life presents, including clear commands and instructions. But rather than that reality leading to discomfort, fear, or anxiety, allow it to operate as a loving safeguard, designed to train and lead you according to His will.

Alongside the Word, the Holy Spirit teaches us directly. Jesus assured us that the Spirit would remind us of everything He taught (**John 14:26**) and guide us into all truth (**John 16:13**). This declaration is re-enforced in **1 John 2:27**, which tells us that *"his anointing teaches you about all things..."* The Holy Spirit implants thoughts, insights, warnings, and ideas, not randomly, but intentionally, so we can stay on the path that He has prepared for us.

The Israelites illustrate the principle of disobedience and delay vividly. They complained about hardship, rejected God's provision, and hesitated to enter the Promised Land because of fear. As a result, God delayed their entry into the Promised Land for forty years so the rebellious generation would die in the wilderness. *"I swear that none of you will enter the land I promised to settle you in, except Caleb son of Jephunneh and Joshua son of Nun."* (**Numbers 14:30**). Many times, we do the same. We delay our blessings, opportunities, and breakthroughs by refusing to trust what God said. But notice Caleb's outcome. **Numbers 14:24** says, *"But since my servant Caleb had a different spirit and has remained loyal to me, I will bring him into the land where he has gone, and his descendants will inherit it."* Caleb moved in faith, obeyed God immediately, and was rewarded with the promise. God will always honor obedience. If you want to walk with God and see His plans unfold in your life with clarity and momentum, choose obedience, because obedience accelerates, and disobedience delays. God will reward your faith.

<u>**[Stop and Read**: Numbers 14:1–35]</u>

## #6. Question Your Motives

One of the most critical disciplines in walking with God is learning to examine *why* you do what you do, and why you *want* to do something. **Proverbs 16:2** reminds us, *"All a person's ways seem right to him, but the Lord weighs* *motives."* We justify our decisions easily, but God looks deeper, beyond the action to the intention. **Proverbs 16:25** adds, *"There is a way that seems right to a person, but its end is the way to death."* In other words, our perceptions can deceive us. It is important to truly be honest with yourself and recognize when your perspective and decisions are not driven by a pure heart. With the help of the Holy Spirit, you can learn to identify when your motivations are not of God, such as fear, selfish ambition, pride, anger, greed, revenge, or unforgiveness, rather than rooted in what is godly, like generosity, faith, forgiveness, humility, patience, and love. This awareness will help guide you in the right direction. Motives matter.

### [<u>Stop and Read</u>: Proverbs 16:1-33]

We see this clearly in the very first sin. Eve's downfall began with a motive she never questioned. **Genesis 3:6** tells us she *"saw the tree was good for food and delightful to look at, and that it was desirable for obtaining wisdom."* Her desire was rooted in distrust of God's Word and disbelief in His provision. She wanted something *outside* of what God approved, because she didn't fully trust what God had already provided. She was motivated by wanting more for herself despite the consequences (selfish ambition). The same is true today. What decisions are you making because you're not fully trusting God's Word or His ability to provide? When you peel back the layers, you'll realize that many decisions stem from hidden motives, such as insecurity, lack of trust in God, fleshly desires, the urge to prove something, or the need to please people instead of pleasing God.

Questioning your motives is essential for discernment. Before making a decision, take some time to ask yourself: *Is this God? Is this the enemy? Or is this just me?* God's voice will always align with truth, love, and righteousness. The enemy's voice will appeal to pride, fear, confusion, and self-gratification. And your own voice will often lean towards comfort, convenience, or self-preservation. It is important to remember that God will never tell you anything that contradicts His Word. And you must know His Word to measure it against your thoughts and motives. God's Word never fails, and when you really believe that and make decisions based on that truth, you will experience better results.

When you examine your motives, your path becomes clearer, your discernment sharper, and your steps more aligned with His will.

## #7. God Watches How We Handle Situations

Developing godly discernment isn't just about hearing God's voice; it's about how we respond when life tests us. **Judges 3:4** tells us, *"The Lord left them to test Israel, to determine if they would keep the Lord's commands."* God intentionally allowed other nations with different beliefs to remain in the Promised Land after the Israelites arrived, to test their obedience and loyalty. He wanted to see if the Israelites would obey Him despite being among nations that worshipped other gods. In the same way, God allows situations, pressures, obstacles, and even temptations to remain in our lives; not to destroy us, but to reveal what's really in our hearts. One important way that God develops us is by exposing how we respond when things don't go the way we planned or want.

This matters deeply for business and life decisions. When a client backs out, a launch flops, finances tighten, or someone mistreats you, how do you react? Do you operate from emotion, fear, frustration, or flesh? Or do you respond according to God's Word? Your reactions reveal whether you are walking in spiritual maturity or instinctively leaning on your own understanding. Discernment grows when we choose obedience in difficulty, not just when everything is smooth.

A powerful and practical way to respond when you face a challenge, setback, or problem is with **the 4 P's**:

1. **Praise and worship God** – Shift your focus from the problem to the One who is greater than the problem. In that moment, honor and worship God with all your might. Give Him glory and praise in the face of adversity. Verbalize it and put your body into it.

2. **Pray in expectation** – Talk to God, believing He will answer, guide, and provide. Thank Him in advance for how He will resolve the

problem and make you better because of it. Talk to Him about the stress and anxiety you may be feeling and your expectations for a solution according to His will.

3. **Pull a promise** – Anchor yourself in Scripture. Speak His Word back to Him and declare the truth over your life and the situation, such as:

   - *"No weapon formed against me shall prosper"* (**Isaiah 54:17**)

   - *"Do not worry about anything, but instead, through prayer and petition, with thanksgiving, present your requests to the Lord, and the peace of God which surpasses all understanding, will guard your hearts and minds in Jesus Christ."* (**Philippians 4:6–7**)

   - *"We know that all things work together for the good of those who love God, who are called according to his purpose."* (**Romans 8:28**)

   - *"Trust in the Lord with all your heart, and lean not on your own understanding, but in all your ways acknowledge Him, and He will direct your paths."* (**Proverbs 3:5–6**)

4. **Proceed** – Trust that God will work it out. Whether it's continuing your day as normal or taking the next bold step that's required to handle the situation.

Then **repeat**.

Every time you choose to respond this way, you train your flesh. You become less reactionary and more Spirit-led. You learn to recognize God's guidance in real time. This is how discernment develops: through repeated obedience in real situations.

If you want God to trust you with bigger assignments, greater influence, more resources, and larger opportunities in business and in life, the Bible reveals that He tests how you handle pressure, disappointment, conflict, and delay. God is watching. Not to punish you, but to prepare you. These tests reveal the places in our hearts that still need surrender, and God invites us to yield to His refining work to produce the character needed to carry His calling on your life. Your response today is shaping your capacity for tomorrow.

The difficult situations God allows you to endure are ultimately for your good. **Judges 3:1–2** explains that when God told the Israelites to inhabit the Promised Land and left combative nations there (instead of clearing them out), it was *"in order to test all those in Israel who had experienced none of the wars in Canaan. This was to teach the future generation of the Israelites how to fight in battle, especially those who had not fought before."* God was not being cruel. He was training them. Without resistance, they would not have developed strength. Without opposition, they would never have learned how to fight. The same is true for us. God allows challenges to remain in our lives to strengthen us and teach us about spiritual warfare, obedience, perseverance, and faith. His training is rarely traditional. He does not prepare us the way the world prepares its leaders. Instead, He teaches us to rely on Him.

[<u>Stop and Read</u>: Judges 2:1-23 and Judges 3:1-11]

Think about the conquest of Jericho. God instructed Joshua and the Israelites to march around the city and shout, a military strategy that appeared to make no sense. (**Joshua 6:1–21**). Yet the city walls fell, and the Israelites conquered Jericho because they obeyed. Or consider Gideon, who faced an army too numerous to count with only 300 men and a handful of horns and jars (**Judges 7:1–23**). By the world's standards, that was a guaranteed loss. But God used obedience, not numbers, to bring victory. The enemy nation turned on themselves, and Israel won a battle that looked impossible. God was training them to trust His voice over their logic.

### [Stop and Read: Joshua 6:1-21]

God trains us in a similar way. Sometimes the strategy He gives you will not look logical. Sometimes He will tell you to launch with less, to move before you feel ready, or to take a step that doesn't make sense on paper. But through these moments, God is developing your spiritual muscles and teaching you to recognize His voice, obey His lead, and fight battles His way, not the world's way. Discernment grows when we learn to see difficulty not as punishment, but as preparation. Every challenge you endure with faith becomes training for the greater things God is calling you to.

## #8. Remember Your Help

As you walk with God, never forget that you are not doing this in your own strength. Under the New Covenant, God has given you the greatest helper: the Holy Spirit. He leads, guides, strengthens, convicts, equips, and empowers you to make godly decisions in every area of life, including business. Discernment becomes clearer when you rely on Him instead of relying solely on your own reasoning. But the Holy Spirit is not your only resource. God has also given you His written Word, the Bible, which serves as your manual for living. Trying to build your life without Scripture is like trying to build a house without the blueprints. You might eventually put something together, but it will be unstable, incomplete, unsafe, and frustrating. The Bible provides the structure, clarity, and guidance needed to build a life that honors God and your divine purpose.

**[<u>Stop and Read</u>: Matthew 7:24-27]**

You must also remember this truth: If God has assigned you, He will find you. You don't have to fight for attention, force opportunities, manipulate people, or elevate yourself. When God calls someone, He knows exactly where they are. David was tending sheep when God chose him. Gideon was hiding in a winepress. Paul was traveling in the wrong direction. God is not limited by your location, your connections, or your visibility. God never gives an assignment without providing the resources, wisdom, relationships, and provision needed to fulfill it. If He ordered it, He will pay for it! Your responsibility is not to strive; it is to surrender. Surrender your timeline, your fears, your need for control, and your desire to prove yourself. Walk in obedience, trust His leading, and remember that everything He asks you to do flows from one foundation: God loves you. His guidance is rooted in love, His correction is rooted in love, and His plans for you are rooted in love. When you remember your help, you will walk with confidence, peace, and discernment, knowing that God Himself is *in* you every step of the way.

"Let love be without hypocrisy. Detest
evil; cling to what is good."

Romans 12:9

# LOVE GOD, LOVE PEOPLE, AND CHOOSE GOOD OVER EVIL

# PART IV

## Love God, Love People, and Choose Good Over Evil

**The Dream**

In the beginning of 2025, I had a dream that changed my life. In the dream, I was with God, and He revealed something so simple, yet so powerful, that instantly soothed my doubt about whether it was even possible to adhere to (what felt like) the complexities of Christianity. He showed me that if we focus on **two things**, everything else in life will fall into place: **#1 Love God and love people, and #2 Choose good over evil.** The moment that truth was revealed in my dream, I felt the greatest euphoria imaginable. It's difficult to describe in words and do it justice. It was as if I had just won the ultimate game show, with confetti bursting around me, gold and bright lights surrounding me, and a joy so pure it overwhelmed every part of my being. It was bliss. Complete, overwhelming, and perfect.

But that remarkable and unforgettable feeling lasted only a split second. It was suddenly snatched away, and in my spirit, I knew exactly why. As the short dream continued, I sensed immediately that the enemy did not want me to grasp what God had just revealed. He did not want that truth rooted in my heart, because he knew the power and freedom that would follow. In an instant, the euphoria vanished and I woke up. Yet as I opened my eyes, I found myself smiling. I could still feel the residue of that heavenly joy, and I knew, deep in my spirit, that what God showed me was true. Love God and love people. Choose good over evil. Everything else flows from those foundations, and the Bible teaches us how to live this out. I'll start with choosing good over evil.

## Choose Good Over Evil

**2 Corinthians 10:3-5** makes it clear that *"For although we live in the flesh, we do not wage war according to the flesh, since the weapons of our warfare are not of the flesh, but are powerful through God for the demolition of strongholds. We demolish arguments and every proud thing that is raised up against the knowledge of God, and we take every thought captive to obey Christ."*

Evil is real, and we need to have a healthy vigilance against it. Oftentimes, it begins with our thoughts. It's our responsibility to recognize when we have thoughts that are not of God, surrender them to Christ, and replace them with the truth. We must capture evil within us when it is in the form of thoughts, including thoughts about ourselves and about others, before they turn into beliefs and actions. The Word of God helps us to know the difference between godly thoughts and those of the enemy.

**James 4:2–8** (pause and read it) confronts us directly. Many people desire things they don't have and resort to fighting, manipulating, or striving, yet still fall short because their motives are wrong. This Scripture warns that friendship with the world makes us enemies of God. The world normalizes sin—strife, fornication, drunkenness, idolatry—and because it's everywhere, it becomes hard to recognize. We conform to the world, and then wonder why our lives aren't fruitful. Many times, the challenges we face are the result of our own actions or inactions (i.e. sinful behavior and disobedience).

**It's our responsibility to recognize when we have thoughts that are not of God, surrender them to Christ, and replace them with the truth.**

God allows these difficulties out of love, to teach, prepare, and refine us. I've identified three parts of this refinement.

1. **To fix our behavior** - This requires a lot of humility and self-awareness. You must be honest with yourself and identify areas in your life that you have not submitted to God. What actions, behaviors, and beliefs do you partake in that are driven by selfishness, pride, unforgiveness, or lack of faith? What

behaviors do you have that you know are not pleasing to God, but you do it anyway? Prioritize fixing all behaviors (yes all) that are not rooted in love. Understand that this is not a one-time thing, but is a life-long commitment.

2.  **To build our relationship with Him** - To develop any relationship, we need to spend time with that person. The same goes for building a relationship with God. Get to know Him and how He operates His kingdom on earth. I've found that the Old Testament teaches a lot about the character of God, how He thinks, what He likes, what He doesn't like, and His intentions. Although we could never confine God or fully understand Him, reading the Bible helps us learn who He is and what He's like. Then, once you get to know Him intimately, you will be able to recognize Him in your everyday life. You can't recognize someone you don't know. He's here. Relationship with God evolves into trust, faith, and dependency on Him.

3.  **To train us** – We are reminded in **Hebrews 12:11** that, *"No discipline seems enjoyable at the time, but painful. Later on, however, it yields the peaceful fruit of righteousness to those who have been trained by it."* It is not uncommon for God to put His loved ones through a challenging time for training. When God wants to teach us something, He must first get our attention and bring us to Him. Unfortunately, for many, the gentle nudge is regularly ignored, so God shakes us up to bring us to Him. He allows us to endure difficult times so that we can be trained by it, showing us that if we trust in Him and prioritize obedience over everything else, we will make it through, be restored, and be even better than before. Once you make it through enough storms better than you expected by trusting God, you will be conditioned to know that *this too shall pass,* and you will gain way more than you think you lost. The question is, how many storms will it take for you to be trained. (*Ooh! I feel the Holy Spirit on that!*)

The storm won't feel easy, but focus on what you *can* control, such as your thoughts, your decisions, and your behaviors. Choosing good over evil is not just a rule; it is the pathway to peace, purpose, and a life aligned with God. When we align our lives with loving God, loving people, and choosing good over evil, everything else really does begin to fall into place. But in order to choose good over evil, we have to know what God considers good and what God says is evil.

## Identify What is Evil and Wicked

The Bible does not leave us guessing about what is evil or wicked. God speaks plainly. Scripture consistently shows us that evil does not begin externally; it originates in the heart. Jesus makes this unmistakably clear in **Mark 7:21–23** when He explains that *"from within, out of people's hearts, come evil thoughts, sexual immoralities, thefts, murders, adulteries, greed, evil actions, deceit, self-indulgence, envy, slander, pride, and foolishness. All these evil things come from within and defile a person."* These things defile a person not because of outside influence alone, but because the heart has not been surrendered and renewed. This is why discernment begins internally. If we are not honest about what is happening in our hearts, we will struggle to recognize what is pulling us away from God.

Paul reinforces this truth repeatedly in his letters to believers in the early church. These letters are a part of what are known as the "Epistles" of the Bible. In **Colossians 3:5–9**, believers are commanded to *"put to death what belongs to your earthly nature: sexual immorality, impurity, lust, evil desire, and greed, which is idolatry."* Added to that list is *"anger, wrath, malice, slander, and filthy language."* These were once the patterns of our old life, but no longer belong to who we are in Christ.

**Romans 1:28–32** paints an even starker picture of what happens when people refuse to acknowledge God: minds become corrupted, and behaviors spiral into unrighteousness, greed, envy, quarrels, deceit, malice, gossip, slander, arrogance, pride, boastfulness, disobedience to parents, unmercifulness, and even celebrating what God calls evil. These verses are sobering because they show how easily sin becomes normalized, and even applauded, when truth is rejected.

**Galatians 5:19–21** continues this warning, listing the works of the flesh as *"sexual immorality, moral impurity, promiscuity, idolatry, sorcery, hatreds, strife, jealousy, outbursts of anger, selfish ambitions, dissensions, factions, envy, drunkenness, carousing, and anything similar,"* stating plainly that those who practice such things will not inherit the kingdom of God. These Scriptures are not meant to condemn us, but to awaken us. They serve to sharpen our discernment so we can recognize what is evil and not of God, keeping in mind that engaging in these behaviors and mindsets invite struggle and permit havoc.

**[<u>Stop and Read</u>: Mark 7:21-23; Colossians 3:5-9; Romans 1:28-32, and Galatians 5:19-21]**

Many times, we engage in these behaviors without even realizing that Scripture identifies them as evil, wicked, or sinful. Things like gossip, drunkenness, quarrels, disobedience to parents, or subtle forms of idolatry can feel "normal" because they are common in everyday life. Other times, we knowingly participate in behaviors but deny that they are wrong, like sexual immorality, excessive partying, or showing little mercy to others, because culture has reframed them as acceptable or harmless. And sometimes we convince ourselves that *a little* of something is okay: a small lie, occasional gossip, pride disguised as confidence, or drinking just enough to blur judgment. But Scripture is clear. **1 Thessalonians 5:22** instructs us to *"stay away from every kind of evil,"* not just the versions that feel extreme or obvious.

There are also areas where we know something is wrong, but we struggle with it because it has become a stronghold. Sexual sin, addiction, strife, recurring drunkenness, and idolatry don't usually take root overnight. They are built brick by brick through repeated lies, justifications, and compromises. But the same way strongholds are built is the same way they are torn down: brick by brick, through truth, repentance, obedience, and the power of the Holy Spirit. Freedom is not found in pretending something isn't wrong. It is found in agreeing with God and allowing Him to heal and restore us.

This is why discernment matters. Without discernment, we risk calling what is wrong, acceptable and remaining bound in the very things God desires to free us from. We must be able to recognize what God considers evil and wicked, and intentionally align our lives to turn away from those things. And when we slip, because we are human, we return quickly through confession and repentance.

This list is not exhaustive, and it's not meant to be legalistic. The Holy Spirit will speak to you personally, bringing conviction and clarity about additional areas in *your* life. Conviction is not condemnation. It is an invitation to freedom.

**Romans 6:21** says "*So what fruit was produced then from the things you are now ashamed of? The outcomes of those things is death.*" It is important to be honest with yourself about your thoughts and behaviors that are not of God, understanding that there are real consequences to disregarding Him. As you learn to recognize what pulls you away from God, and respond by choosing differently, your spiritual discernment sharpens, your walk grows stronger, and your life begins to reflect the peace and power that God designed for you.

## Choosing Good

While Scripture clearly identifies what must be put away, it is just as clear about what we are called to *put on*.

**Colossians 3:12–16** reminds us that we are God's chosen ones, holy and dearly loved, and because of that identity, our lives should reflect *"compassion, kindness, humility, gentleness, and patience, bearing with one another and forgiving one another…"* as we have been forgiven. Above all, we are instructed to *"put on love, which is the perfect bond of unity."* God's way is to *"let the peace of Christ rule your hearts. And be thankful."*

When we choose these virtues, the peace of Christ is allowed to rule in our hearts, and gratitude becomes our posture. These Scriptures tells us that letting the Word of God dwell richly within us shapes not only how we think, but how we treat others, how we worship, and how we live daily. As the Word takes root in our hearts, it transforms us into people who reflect the character of Christ in both our inner lives and our outward actions.

**[<u>Stop and Read</u>: Colossians 3:12-17]**

This way of life requires intentionality and humility. **Philippians 2:3–4** instructs us to *"consider others more important than yourselves,"* looking not to our own interests but to the interests of others.

Even our attitude matters. **Philippians 2:14** instructs us to *"Do everything without grumbling and arguing."* **1 Thessalonians 5:16–18** adds another layer: *"Rejoice always, pray constantly, give thanks in everything."* This is not situational obedience. It is a lifestyle rooted in gratitude, faith, and trust. **Hebrews 13:5** further grounds us, stating *"Keep your life free from the love of money. Be satisfied with what you have,"* because God Himself promises never to leave or forsake us. Discernment grows when our decisions are not driven by greed, comparison, or fear, but by contentment and confidence in God's presence and provision.

Our words and conduct are also part of choosing good. **Ephesians 4:29** warn us that *"No foul language should come from your mouth, but only what is good for building up someone in need."* We are instructed in **Ephesians 4:32** to *"be kind and compassionate to one another, forgiving one another, just as God also forgave you in Christ."* **Hebrews 12:1–2 & 14** ties it all together by reminding us to *"run with endurance the race that lies before us, keeping our eyes on Jesus, the pioneer and perfecter of our faith"* while instructing us to actively *"Pursue peace with everyone, and holiness—"* The Greek word for "run" used in **Hebrews 12:1** is *trechō,* which is metaphorically used to signify exerting one's effort. This illustrates that we are on a path that demands focus, discipline, and resilience. The fruit of godly discernment is a life that reflects Christ in how we think, speak, and live, choosing what is right, even when it costs us comfort or convenience. In doing so, we remain grounded, guarded, and guided by truth, staying aligned with the path and purpose God has designed for us.

Choosing good is not vague or subjective. It is demonstrated through attitudes, behaviors, and heart postures that reflect the character of Christ. According to God's Word, we are to be *obedient,* responding quickly and willingly to His instruction. We are called to be *compassionate* and *kind*, extending grace to others the same way God extends grace to us. *Humility*, *gentleness*, and *patience* are marks of spiritual maturity, shaping how we interact with people, especially in difficult moments. God also calls us to be *forgiving*, releasing offense while choosing *mercy*, and to live with a *thankful* and *grateful* heart, recognizing that everything we have comes from Him.

God considers it good when we walk in *wisdom*, making decisions that honor Him rather than ourselves. He calls us to *consider the needs of others above our own*, to be *peaceful*, and to *live content*, satisfied with what He has provided instead of constantly striving for more outside of Him. *Endurance* matters to God, continuing in *faith* even when the journey is long or uncomfortable. He instructs us to *pursue holiness*, not perfection, but a life set apart for Him. And above all, He calls us to *set our minds on things above*, not on earthly things, anchoring our thoughts, priorities, and desires in eternity. When we adopt these characteristics as our standard of living, discernment becomes clearer, our walk with God deepens, and our lives begin to reflect the goodness of the One we follow.

As you learn what God considers good, it is essential to understand where that clarity comes from. You must read the Word of God for yourself; not just hear it from sermons, social media clips, or other people's interpretations. Hearing the Word is powerful, but engaging with the Word personally is transformational. When you open the Bible and spend time with it, God reveals truth directly to you. His words become alive, personal, and timely. Scripture stops being information and becomes instruction, correction, comfort, and direction for your life.

God makes this promise clear in **Joshua 1:8**: *"This book of instruction must not depart from your mouth; you are to meditate on it day and night so that you may carefully observe everything written in it. For then, you will prosper and have success in whatever you do."* Prosperity and success (biblically defined) flow from knowing, meditating on, and

> Hearing the Word is powerful, but engaging the Word personally is transformational.

obeying God's Word. Discernment is sharpened when Scripture shapes your thinking, your choices, and your reactions. The more time you spend in the Word, the more easily you recognize what is good, what is off, and what God is calling you to do next.

**The Enemy Comes to Steal, Kill, and Destroy**

However, Scripture is clear that there is opposition to this way of life. Jesus warned us plainly in **John 10:10**: *"The thief comes only to steal and kill and destroy."* Any time you are pursuing truth, obedience, and discernment, the enemy will attempt to interfere. We see this pattern from the very beginning in **Genesis 3:1–7**, in the Garden of Eden.

<u>**[Stop and Read**: Genesis 3:1-7]</u>

From this passage, we are taught about Satan's schemes:

1. **He disguises himself** – Satan did not appear as an obvious enemy. He disguised himself as a creature that belonged in the garden.

This likely disarmed Eve, making it appear safe to engage.

2. **He tries to make you doubt what you heard God say** – His strategy was subtle. He questioned what God had said, planting doubt where certainty once existed.

3. **He says the opposite of God's Word** – In speaking to Eve, Satan twisted God's words and outright contradicted them, saying: *"No, you will certainly not die"* (**Genesis 3:4**), when clearly God said, *"for on the day you eat from it, you will certainly die."* (**Genesis 2:17**).

4. **He wants you to believe that you're lacking and don't have enough** – Adam and Eve had everything in the Garden of Eden. God abundantly provided for them, and they literally lacked nothing. They lived in the perfection that God created and intended for all of us. But Satan's encounter deceitfully suggested that Eve was missing something (wisdom, power, fulfillment) even though she had everything.

5. **He tempts you to give into your fleshly cravings** – Satan tapped into one of the primary desires of the body: food and taste. Surely by then, they learned that food satisfies the body and that fruit is delicious.

In response to Satan, Eve initially repeated what God said, but when the enemy pushed back, she gave in. The moment she shifted from trusting God's Word to trusting her own reasoning, deception took hold.

The same tactics are still used today. The enemy tries to make you doubt what you know God told you, like *start the business*, *leave the relationship*, or *make the move*. Satan whispers that you don't have enough money, experience, time, or resources. He convinces you that obedience will cost too much, and disobedience will cost nothing. These lies are designed to pull you away from faith and into fear, passivity, or compromise.

Thankfully, Jesus' temptation in **Matthew 4:1–11** shows us how to respond.

## [<u>Stop and Read</u>: Matthew 4:1-11 and compare to Adam and Eve's response]

Satan tried the same schemes with Jesus: questioning His identity (*"If you are the Son of God…"*), tempting Him when He was physically weak, misapplying Scripture, offering worldly luxuries, and encouraging Him to skip the process by taking the crown without the cross. But unlike Adam and Eve, Jesus fought back with truth. He did not debate, reason, or explain. He responded with the Word of God, correctly applied and firmly believed.

This contrast teaches us a powerful lesson: discernment is not passive and knowing Scripture is not enough. **You must speak it and stand on it**. The enemy will always try to distort truth, but when you recognize his schemes and respond with God's Word, you protect your calling, your peace, and your progress.

**Fight Back**

The difference between how Eve and Jesus responded to Satan's attempts is clear. Jesus fought back. Not with fists, aggression, or arrogance, but with the Word of God. Spiritual warfare is not always dramatic. It is daily and intentional, both rooted in and agitated by truth. The first and most important weapon is the Word of God. Lies are only defeated by truth, and truth must be known to be used. This is why reading the Bible for yourself matters so deeply. The more truth you know, the easier it is to discern a lie. When the enemy whispers doubt, fear, lack, or compromise, you must counter it with what God has already said. Jesus did not argue with Satan emotionally or intellectually. He responded with Scripture. If you don't know the Word of God, you won't recognize when it's being twisted, and you won't know how to respond when deception shows up.

A major part of fighting back is *talking* back. Silence is not humility when you're under spiritual attack—it's surrender to the enemy. Jesus said plainly, *"Go away, Satan."* He rebuked, commanded, and shut the conversation down. You are empowered to do the

> **Lies are only defeated by truth, and truth must be known to be used.**

same. When thoughts come that contradict God's Word, such as: *You're not ready. You don't have enough. This won't work. Did God really say...* you must confront them out loud. Rebuke the lie and replace it with the truth. Declare what God said. And then repeat. Jesus said, in **John 8:31-32**, *"If you continue in my word, you really are my disciples. You will know the truth, and the truth will set you free."*

**Silence is not humility when you're under spiritual attack– it's surrender to the enemy.**

Warfare is not a one-time event; it's persistent. The enemy often leaves for a season and comes back looking for another opening. Discernment keeps you alert.

**2 Corinthians 10:5** tells us exactly how to live this out: *"we take every thought captive to obey Christ."* That means you do not allow every thought to sit, linger, or influence your decisions. You evaluate it. You question it. You measure it against Scripture.

Our thoughts are seeds. They either produce fruit of the Spirit, or weeds of the enemy. You must not let the enemy plant seeds of doubt, fear, offense, hate, or pride in your mind. The key is to recognize it and uproot it **immediately**. Then, force yourself (because it won't be easy) to plant a seed of love in its place. This is an example of what that process looks like:

You help a friend by letting her live in your home for a few months, but soon your friend starts doing things that appear to take advantage of your kindness. For the first time, you and your friend get into an argument. You go to your room and start having thoughts about how ungrateful your friend is and that you should have never let her stay with you in the first place. Boom! That's the seed of the enemy. The first step is to recognize that it's not a thought from God, our loving Savior who, through His Word says, *"Whatever you do, do it from the heart, as something done for the Lord and not for people"* (**Colossians 3:23**). Even if you can't pull that Scripture in the moment, you know that God is love, and those thoughts you're having are not loving thoughts. So, you replace them, and you force yourself to say and repeat out loud something like: "Thank you, Lord, that you gave me a home to even be able to share with someone else. Thank you, Lord, that you trusted me to help serve your purpose in my friend's life. Thank you, God, for your peace which surpasses all understanding. God, you are good, and I know that I will learn, grow, develop, and be better because of these circumstances." And pray for your friend. It's pretty hard to be upset with someone that you pray for. After that, you will see that you start to feel lighter and not as upset. You've uprooted (or started to uproot) the seed. Repeat this process as many times as needed. It works, and it gets easier once you start to see the divine results it brings.

It's important to recognize when fear is trying to drive your business decisions, when insecurity is shaping your relationships, or when pride is influencing your reactions. This is war, and it's personal. You must declare to the enemy, "You're not going to get me! You're not going to steal my peace, my obedience, my calling, or my future!" When you fight with truth, authority, and consistency, discernment becomes second nature, and the enemy loses ground every time.

## Be Vigilant

Scripture gives a clear warning: *"Don't give the devil an opportunity"* (**Ephesians 4:27**). The enemy cannot force his way into your life. He looks for open doors. These doors are often created through everyday choices that seem harmless but slowly compromise spiritual awareness. The people we keep close, the places we frequent, the entertainment we consume, and even how we engage on social media all matter. Balance is key, but awareness is essential. You must protect yourself from outside influences that taint your clarity and obstruct your channel with God.

The enemy frequently uses what we *see* to lure us. In **Genesis 3:6**, Eve *"saw that the tree was good and delightful to **look at**,"* and her eyes became the gateway to deception. In **Matthew 4:8**, the Bible says *"the devil took him to a very high mountain and **showed** him all the kingdoms of the world"* illustrating Satan's attempt to entice Jesus through visual temptation. What you allow before your eyes can either strengthen discernment or dull it.

Habits also open doors, especially those that weaken self-control and spiritual sensitivity. Substance abuse, uncontrolled emotions, and even unhealthy dating habits can distort judgment and pull you away from God's best. Discernment is critical here, because the wrong relationships and influence can derail purpose faster than almost anything else. Even more serious are patterns of sin and disobedience, which invite chaos rather than peace. Drunkenness, sexual immorality, lying, strife, pride, idolatry, and a lack of love for others do not just affect behavior, they affect spiritual clarity. These choices cloud discernment, weaken resistance, and create space for confusion and turmoil. Walking with God requires conscious and active effort. When you close the doors that the enemy looks for, you protect your peace, preserve your discernment, and position yourself to hear God's voice clearly.

Walking with discernment also requires vigilance. Scripture does not tell us to be passive. It tells us to be prepared. **Ephesians 6:11–17** commands believers to:

*"Put on the full armor of God so that you can stand against the schemes of the devil. For our struggle is not against flesh and blood, but against the rulers, against the authorities, against the cosmic powers of this darkness, against evil, spiritual forces in the heavens. For this reason take up the full armor of God, so that you may be able to resist in the evil day, and having prepared everything, to take your stand. Stand, therefore, with **truth** like a belt around your waist, **righteousness** like armor on your chest, and your feet sandaled with readiness for the gospel of **peace**. In every situation take up the shield of **faith** with which you can extinguish all the flaming arrows of the evil one. Take the helmet of **salvation** and the sword of the Spirit — which is the **word of God**."*

This reminds us that our struggles are not merely human or circumstantial; they are spiritual. Because of that, we must be armed spiritually every day. God provides everything we need to stand firm, resist temptation, and remain clear-minded in the face of opposition. Each piece of the armor plays a vital role:

- **The Belt of Truth** holds everything together. When lies arise, we replace them with the truth of God's Word.

- **The Breastplate of Righteousness** protects the heart and is not earned by performance, but received through faith in Jesus and lived out by following His example.

- **The Gospel of Peace** steadies us, allowing us to remain content and secure even in troubled seasons, knowing we are right with God and assured of our salvation.

- **The Shield of Faith** guards us when doubts, fears, or accusations are thrown our way, reminding us that God is the creator and ruler of all things, and will do what He promised.

- **The Helmet of Salvation** protects the mind, anchoring us in the truth that Jesus has already freed us from condemnation.

- **The Sword of the Spirit**, which is the Word of God and our offensive weapon. This is how we fight back. We operate in the Spirit, not in the flesh, using God's Word to confront lies, temptation, and deception.

This responsibility to stand guard is presented in **Genesis 4:7**, when God warns Cain: *"If you do what is right, won't you be accepted? But if you do not do what is right, sin is crouching at the door. Its desire is for you, but you must rule over it."*

In Hebrew, the word "accepted" as used in **Genesis 4:7** is *śə'ēṯ* (pronounced *seh-ayth'*), and carries the meaning of "being lifted up or exalted." In other words, God reveals in the Scripture that obedience elevates us. Many times, chaos enters our lives not because the enemy is overpowering, but because we fail to rule over sin through obedience to the Word of God. Jesus has already made the ultimate sacrifice for that rulership, once and for all. **Hebrews 10:12** tells us *"But this man, after offering one sacrifice for sins forever, sat down at the right hand of God."* The work is finished and paid in full. The authority has been given. Now it is time to take your power back! Use what you know. Walk in the authority Christ has given to you. Choose good over evil. Stand firm and rule over sin, instead of letting it rule over you.

## Love God and Love People

When I woke up from the dream where God revealed the two foundations: **(1) love God and love people, and (2) choose good over evil**, one thought stayed with me. Sometimes the Christian life can feel like there is so much to remember. There are commands, disciplines, warnings, and instructions throughout Scripture. But Jesus simplifies it. Beneath everything is one foundation: love.

In **Matthew 22:36–40**, Jesus was asked which commandment in the law was the greatest. His answer cut through every religious complexity: *"Love the Lord your God with all your heart, with all your soul, and with all your mind. This is the greatest and most important command. The second is like it: Love your neighbor as yourself. All the Law and the Prophets depend on these two commands."* Every instruction

God gives flows from this foundation. If you love God fully and love people genuinely, your actions, decisions, and responses will naturally begin to align with His will.

**1 John 4:7-8** expands this truth even further: *"Dear friends, let us love one another, because love is from God, and everyone who loves has been born of God and knows God. The one who does not love does not know God, because God is love."* Love is not simply an emotion or personality trait. It is the very nature of God Himself. God demonstrated this love by emptying Himself and assuming the form of a servant, taking on the likeness of humanity and becoming a man, humbling himself through obedience to the point of death and resurrection so that we could no longer be enslaved to sin, but gifted with grace! Thank you, Jesus!

**[Stop and Read: 1 John 4:7-21, Philippians 2:5-11, and Romans 6:1-23]**

Because God loved us first, we are now called to love others in the same way. The Scriptures even say that if someone claims to love

God but hates their brother or sister, that claim is not genuine (**1 John 4:20**). Our love for God must be visible in how we treat people.

This kind of love also produces freedom. **1 John 4:18** explains that *"...perfect love drives out fear..."* God is the only one that has perfect love, so when we truly understand that God loves us and find security in Him, fear loses its power. Fear of rejection, fear of failure, fear of loss, and fear of judgment begin to dissolve in the presence of God's love. Love becomes the evidence that God remains in us and that His Spirit is at work in our lives.

**1 John 5:3** tells us that *"For this is what love for God is: to keep His commands. And his commands are not a burden."* Therefore, love, as the Bible describes it, is far deeper than a feeling. Feelings come and go, but biblical love is a decision expressed through obedience to God. Scripture makes this clear: loving God means keeping His commands. Love is not measured by emotion or words alone. It is revealed through how we live, how we treat others, and the choices we make.

**[<u>Stop and Read</u>: 1 John 5:1-4]**

Love shows itself in everyday actions. Love chooses to be compassionate toward others, even when they are difficult to understand. Love practices kindness and patience, resisting the urge to react harshly. Love walks in humility and gentleness, recognizing that we are all dependent on God's grace. Love cultivates a grateful heart, chooses to forgive, and seeks to live in peace rather than conflict. Love also pursues holiness, desiring to live in a way that reflects God's character and honors His presence within us.

At the same time, love requires restraint. Love refuses to indulge in what God calls harmful or destructive. It turns away from greed, pride, envy, lust, wrath, filthy language, lying, sexual immorality, strife, selfish ambition, and lack of mercy. These things damage relationships, cloud discernment, and pull us away from the life God intends. Choosing love means intentionally rejecting behaviors that harm ourselves or others.

Scripture contains much more guidance about how love should shape our lives. That is why it is essential to read the Bible for yourself. The more you immerse yourself in God's Word, the more clearly you will understand what love looks like in action. As the Holy Spirit teaches you through Scripture, love stops being an abstract idea and becomes the foundation for how you think, speak, and live each day.

We often underestimate the power of love. We think strength looks like control, intelligence, influence, or strategy. But in God's kingdom, love is the most powerful force that exists. Love aligns our hearts with God, shapes our relationships with others, and becomes the foundation for every decision we make. God *is* love. When love becomes your foundation, discernment becomes clearer, obedience becomes lighter, and the life God designed for you begins to unfold the way it was always meant to.

## A New Life

Following Christ is not simply adopting a new set of beliefs. It is stepping into an entirely new life. It brings new habits, new character, and a new way of seeing the world. This transformation is what Jesus meant when He said we must be born again. In **John 3:3**, Jesus says, *"Truly I tell you, unless someone is born again, he cannot see the kingdom of God."* Notice that He says *see* the kingdom. The kingdom of God exists whether we recognize it or not, but until our hearts are renewed, we cannot perceive it. When you are truly born again, something within you changes. Your spiritual eyes open. You begin to see life, choices, challenges, people, and circumstances through a completely different lens, and you feel that you can no longer be the same as you were.

Jesus continues this explanation in **John 3:5–6**: *"unless someone is born of water and the Spirit, he cannot enter the kingdom of God. Whatever is born of flesh is flesh, and whatever is born of Spirit is spirit."* Our first birth is natural. We are born into families, cultures, traditions, and influences that shape how we think and live. Our parents, caretakers, and environment help direct our habits, values, and identity. But when we are born again in Christ, we experience a spiritual birth. The Spirit of God begins to guide our decisions, reshape our desires, and influence our character. Instead of living primarily from the impulses of the flesh, we begin to reflect the identity and authority of the Holy Spirit within us.

I remember when it finally clicked for me what Jesus meant when He said in **Matthew 16:25**, *"For whoever wants to save his life will lose it, but whoever loses his life because of me will find it."* My carnal mind didn't understand why Jesus would want me to lose my life. But when my spiritual eyes were opened through confession, repentance, and truly seeking God for myself, one day I finally understood. The life we try to control, preserve, and build on our own terms will never lead to true fulfillment. It is only in surrender and laying down our plans, methods, and sense of control that we discover the life He has always intended for us. Losing your life for Him is not loss at all, but an exchange for something far greater: purpose, peace, provision, and eternal significance. When you choose obedience over comfort, and faith over fear, you step into a life that is full, anchored, and led by God. This is where true life is found. Not in holding on, but in fully letting go.

This new life does not happen overnight, but it begins the moment we surrender to Christ. Day by day, as we read Scripture, pray, obey, and allow the Holy Spirit to lead us, our lives begin to reflect God's nature more clearly. The old patterns slowly lose their hold, and a new pattern of living emerges, rooted in truth, discernment, obedience, and love. This is what it truly means for you to be born again! **Ephesians 2:1-5** explains *"And you were dead in your trespasses and sins in which you previously walked according to the ways of this world, according to the ruler of the power of the air, the spirit now working in the disobedient. We too all previously lived among them in our fleshly desires, carrying out the inclinations of our flesh and thoughts, and we were by nature children under wrath as the others were also. **But God**, who is rich in mercy, because of his great love that he had for us, made us alive with Christ even though we were dead in trespasses. You are saved by grace!"*

Praise God!

# THE COMMISSION

Throughout this journey, we have explored a path to strengthen your godly discernment. We began with the foundation of understanding God's kingdom and His covenant with humanity. We saw how the Old Covenant revealed God's standards and how the New Covenant, through Jesus Christ, opened the door for forgiveness, transformation, and eternal life. Through Christ's sacrifice and resurrection, we are reconciled to God and invited into a restored relationship with Him.

From there, we learned that salvation is not just about being rescued, but it is about living differently. Jesus is not only our Savior, but also our

Lord, and that means surrendering our lives to His leadership. Confession, repentance, and obedience become part of our daily walk. And we are not left to navigate this life alone. God gives us the Holy Spirit, who lives within believers as our helper, teacher, and guide.

We also examined the characteristics of walking with God: trusting His timing and His plan, moving when He tells us to move, recognizing that His plans may not always make sense to us, considering our motives, responding faithfully in difficult situations, and remembering the help He provides through His Word and Spirit. These principles cultivate the spiritual sensitivity needed to make wise decisions in life, relationships, and business.

Discernment also requires awareness of spiritual warfare. The enemy seeks to steal, kill, and destroy (**John 10:10**), using deception, temptation, and distraction. But Scripture equips us to stand firm. By putting on the full armor of God, guarding our thoughts, resisting sin, and responding with truth, we can close the doors the enemy looks for and walk confidently in the authority Christ has given us.

At the center of everything is a simple yet powerful truth: love God and love people. Jesus taught that all of God's commands rest on these two foundations. Love is not merely a feeling. Love is expressed through obedience, humility, kindness, forgiveness, and a commitment to pursue holiness while turning away from evil. When love becomes the guiding principle of our lives, our decisions naturally align with God's will.

But this transformation is not meant to stop with us. Jesus gave His followers a clear mission known as the Great Commission. In **Matthew 28:19–20**, Jesus said: *"Therefore go and make disciples of all nations, baptizing them in the name of the Father and of the Son and of the Holy Spirit, and teaching them to obey everything I have commanded you. And surely I am with you always, to the very end of the age."* As born-again believers, we are not called to keep the goodness of God, the truth of His Word, and the glory of His transformation to ourselves. We are commissioned to share it with others. Our personal reformation is meant to lead to the transformation of others. The wisdom, discernment, and freedom God develops in us become tools to help guide, encourage, and disciple those around us.

The journey of discernment does not end here. In many ways, it is just beginning. Each day brings new choices, new challenges, and new opportunities to follow God's way and to reflect His love to others. As you continue to seek Him, immerse yourself in His Word, respond to the Holy Spirit, and walk in obedience, you will grow stronger in wisdom, deeper in faith, and clearer in direction.

And when life feels complicated, remember the revelation that ignited this journey:

**Love God. Love people. Choose good over evil.**

*But seek first the kingdom of God, and his righteousness, and all these things will be provided for you.*

*Matthew 6:33*

# QUESTIONS FOR GROUP DISCUSSION

*Part I: The Covenants and the Gospel*

1. The Old Covenant revealed God's law and the seriousness of sin, while the New Covenant offers forgiveness and transformation through Jesus. How does understanding the purpose of both covenants deepen your appreciation for the Gospel?

______________________________

______________________________

______________________________

______________________________

2. Hebrews explains that the Old Covenant could not remove sin, which is why a better covenant was needed. In what ways does the New Covenant change how we approach God, forgiveness, and righteousness?

______________________________

______________________________

______________________________

______________________________

3. Part One of this book explains that a covenant requires death for a will to take effect, which is why Jesus' sacrifice was necessary. Does this perspective change the way you view the cross and the significance of Christ's death and resurrection? If so, how?

_______________________________________________

_______________________________________________

_______________________________________________

_______________________________________________

_______________________________________________

_______________________________________________

4. After receiving salvation through faith in Jesus, believers are called to live differently. What are some practical ways we can reflect the Gospel in our daily decisions, relationships, and priorities?

_______________________________________________

_______________________________________________

_______________________________________________

_______________________________________________

_______________________________________________

1. The book explains that the Holy Spirit is not just powerful, but *the power of God living within us.* How does recognizing that the Holy Spirit lives in you change the way you approach decisions, challenges, and temptations?

_______________________________________

_______________________________________

_______________________________________

_______________________________________

2. The Holy Spirit requires our attention and often speaks through Scripture, conviction, and subtle promptings. What are some practical ways you can become more intentional about listening to the Holy Spirit in your daily life?

_______________________________________

_______________________________________

_______________________________________

_______________________________________

3. The book discusses how our own desires can sometimes be mistaken for the voice of God if we are not honest about our motives. Why are self-awareness and honesty important when seeking guidance from the Holy Spirit?

_______________________________________

_______________________________________

_______________________________________

_______________________________________

_______________________________________

4. The book describes several characteristics of the Holy Spirit, including that He is God, He lives within believers, He requires our attention, He knows all truth, and He empowers us. Which of these characteristics stood out to you the most, and how might understanding that truth change the way you listen to, rely on, or respond to the Holy Spirit in your daily life?

_______________________________________

_______________________________________

_______________________________________

_______________________________________

1. The book explains that God's timing is often different from ours, using examples like Joseph and David. Why do you think waiting is such an important part of walking with God, and how can we remain faithful during seasons of waiting?

_______________________________________

_______________________________________

_______________________________________

_______________________________________

_______________________________________

2. God often gives direction one step at a time rather than revealing the entire plan. Can you share a time when you felt God leading you but didn't have all the details? How did you respond, and what did you learn from that experience?

_______________________________________

_______________________________________

_______________________________________

_______________________________________

3. God often allows difficult situations to train us, strengthen our faith, and develop our discernment. Can you think of a challenging situation in your life that may have been part of God's preparation rather than punishment? What did that experience teach you about trusting and walking with God?

________________________________________

________________________________________

________________________________________

________________________________________

________________________________________

4. The book teaches that obedience strengthens discernment, and disobedience can delay your promise. What are some practical ways we can grow in obedience so that we can better recognize and follow God's guidance?

________________________________________

________________________________________

________________________________________

________________________________________

________________________________________

1. The Bible teaches that love is not just a feeling but is demonstrated through obedience to God's commands. How does this definition of love challenge or change the way you think about loving God and loving others?

_______________________________________

_______________________________________

_______________________________________

_______________________________________

_______________________________________

2. Scripture lists many behaviors that God considers evil and calls believers to turn away from them. Why do you think some of these behaviors have become normalized in today's culture, and how can we stay spiritually aware of them?

_______________________________________

_______________________________________

_______________________________________

_______________________________________

3. The book suggests that sometimes the difficulties we experience in life may be connected to our own actions or choices. How can examining your own thoughts and behaviors regularly help you to grow in discernment and choose good over evil?

_______________________________________________

_______________________________________________

_______________________________________________

_______________________________________________

_______________________________________________

_______________________________________________

4. Loving people includes showing compassion, patience, humility, forgiveness, and kindness. Which of these qualities do you find most challenging to practice, and what practical steps can you take to grow in that area?

_______________________________________________

_______________________________________________

_______________________________________________

_______________________________________________

_______________________________________________

_______________________________________________

# PERSONAL REFLECTIONS

Do not skip the following personal reflection questions. They are an important part of this journey and a meaningful tool for transformation.

These questions are designed to help you slow down and honestly examine your heart, thoughts, and actions before God. Take time to reflect and write your responses, inviting the Holy Spirit to reveal areas that may need repentance, healing, or growth. This is not about guilt or perfection. It is about drawing closer to God and allowing Him to reveal to you places that need healing, restoration, and revival. As you write and pray through these questions, allow the truth of God's Word to reshape your mindset, decisions, and daily walk with Him.

As you take time for honest reflection, know that bursts of emotion are both normal and healthy. Deep reflection may stir conviction, and also creates space for God to bring relief, healing, and joy.

Write your responses in your personal journal.

1. <u>Heart Examination</u>: What thoughts, attitudes, or behaviors in your life do you know are not aligned with God's Word? Write them down honestly and

bring them before God in prayer, asking the Holy Spirit to help you repent, heal, and change.

2. <u>Motives and Decisions</u>: Think about and write down some of the major decisions you are currently facing in your life, relationships, or work. Through honest self-reflection, identify the underlying motivations that are attracting you to each option, such as faith, fear of lack or failure, obedience, pride, insecurity, the desire for approval from others, etc. How does this list help guide your decision-making?

3. <u>Patterns and Strongholds</u>: Are there patterns, habits, or sins that keep showing up in your life? Write them down. Ask yourself: *What lie have I believed that allowed this pattern to develop?* Then ask the Holy Spirit to replace that lie with God's truth.

4. <u>Mindset</u>: What thoughts regularly occupy your mind? Are they rooted in God's truth, or in worry, comparison, fear, resentment, or self-reliance? Write down the thoughts you struggle with and ask God to help you take those thoughts captive and align them with Christ.

5. <u>Your Walk with God</u>: If someone observed your daily life, including your priorities, conversations, habits, and decisions, what evidence would they see

that you are walking with God? What areas need to change for your life to reflect your faith more clearly?

6. <u>Your Commitment to Transformation</u>: What is one area where the Holy Spirit is currently convicting or challenging you to grow? Write a practical step you will take this week to surrender that area to God and walk in obedience.

7. <u>Spiritual Strength</u>: Galatians 5:22-23 reveals that the fruit of the Spirit is love, joy, peace, patience, kindness, goodness, faithfulness, gentleness, and self-control. Take time to honestly assess these traits within yourself, and rank each of these from strongest to weakest. Write them down in that order. Then, bring your weakest areas before God in prayer, asking the Holy Spirit to strengthen and develop them in you. A few months later, revisit the list and see if the order has changed. Then repeat.

**Congratulations on completing this journey!**

Your willingness to read, reflect, sit with Scripture, and honestly examine your heart is not small. It is evidence of a sincere desire to know God and walk in truth. Every page you turned, every question you answered, and every moment you paused to listen for His voice, matters. This kind of intentional pursuit creates space for real transformation. Be encouraged! What God has begun in you, He is faithful to complete.

Do not stop here. Continue to read your Bible daily and take the Word of God as the ultimate truth. Apply it, speak it, and live it. Surrender your plans, your thoughts, and your desires to Him, trusting that His way is better.

Remember that you are deeply loved by God, and your strength is found in Him. Your call to action is to know the truth, uproot the lies, and choose, every day, to walk faithfully with Him. Let your life reflect His truth, His power, and His love.

# NOTES

If this book stirred something in you, there is more waiting for you.

*Start Now or Stay Still* began as a live, online Bible study series. It's an experience where these teachings come to life through deeper explanation, real-time application, and spiritual insight led by Dayna Thomas. This audio-visual version invites you to not only read the Word, but to hear it taught, see it broken down, and walk through it in a more immersive way.

You are invited to continue your journey.

Access the recordings at:
**LivePaidInFull.com/SNSSClass**

Your next step is waiting.

# ABOUT THE AUTHOR

Dayna Thomas, Esq. is an attorney, entrepreneur, business coach, and founder of *Paid in Full*, a ministry created to help current and aspiring entrepreneurs out of struggle and into purpose through wholehearted surrender and devotion to God.

Dayna's journey began with a bold step of faith—launching her own law firm right out of law school. What started as a leap into the unknown grew into a thriving business law practice serving entrepreneurs across the country. Expanding her impact beyond the traditional practice of law, Dayna later developed online courses that equip entrepreneurs and lawyers with the knowledge and practical strategies needed to start, structure, and grow successful businesses.

Over time, Dayna recognized a deeper calling that extended beyond business to helping people build lives rooted in truth, faith, and purpose. Through *Paid in Full*, she now integrates biblical teaching with practical business guidance, equipping others to build both their lives and businesses on the firm foundation of Jesus Christ. Grounded in surrender, truth, obedience, and unwavering trust in God, her work empowers believers to walk in clarity, courage, and conviction.

Dayna is also the proud mother of one exceptional son, Kamden.

## <u>CONTACT</u>

PAID IN FULL

www.LivePaidInFull.com

For bookings and information, please contact:
info@LivePaidInFull.com

9 798995 418511